THE MERCHANT OF VENICE

William Shakespeare

SPARK PUBLISHING

SPARKNOTES is a registered trademark of SparkNotes LLC

Spark Publishing
A Division of Barnes & Noble
120 Fifth Avenue
New York, NY 10011
www.sparknotes.com

ISBN-13: 978-1-4114-0728-2
ISBN-10: 1-4114-0728-8

Please submit changes or report errors to www.sparknotes.com/errors.

Printed in the United States

10 9 8 7 6 5 4 3 2 1

CONTENTS

CONTEXT

THE MOST INFLUENTIAL WRITER IN ALL OF ENGLISH literature, William Shakespeare was born in 1564 to a successful middle-class glover in Stratford-upon-Avon, England. Shakespeare attended grammar school, but his formal education proceeded no further. In 1582 he married an older woman, Anne Hathaway, and had three children with her. Around 1590 he left his family behind and traveled to London to work as an actor and playwright. Public and critical acclaim quickly followed, and Shakespeare eventually became the most popular playwright in England and part-owner of the Globe Theater. His career bridged the reigns of Elizabeth I (ruled 1558–1603) and James I (ruled 1603–1625), and he was a favorite of both monarchs. Indeed, James granted Shakespeare's company the greatest possible compliment by bestowing upon its members the title of King's Men. Wealthy and renowned, Shakespeare retired to Stratford and died in 1616 at the age of fifty-two. At the time of Shakespeare's death, literary luminaries such as Ben Jonson hailed his works as timeless.

Shakespeare's works were collected and printed in various editions in the century following his death, and by the early eighteenth century, his reputation as the greatest poet ever to write in English was well established. The unprecedented admiration garnered by his works led to a fierce curiosity about Shakespeare's life, but the dearth of biographical information has left many details of Shakespeare's personal history shrouded in mystery. Some people have concluded from this fact and from Shakespeare's modest education that Shakespeare's plays were actually written by someone else—Francis Bacon and the Earl of Oxford are the two most popular candidates—but the support for this claim is overwhelmingly circumstantial, and the theory is not taken seriously by many scholars.

In the absence of credible evidence to the contrary, Shakespeare must be viewed as the author of the thirty-seven plays and 154 sonnets that bear his name. The legacy of this body of work is immense. A number of Shakespeare's plays seem to have transcended even the category of brilliance, becoming so influential as to affect profoundly the course of Western literature and culture ever after.

The Merchant of Venice was probably written in either 1596 or 1597, after Shakespeare had written such plays as *Romeo and Juliet* and *Richard III,* but before he penned the great tragedies of his later years. Its basic plot outline, with the characters of the merchant, the poor suitor, the fair lady, and the villainous Jew, is found in a number of contemporary Italian story collections, and Shakespeare borrowed several details, such the choice of caskets that Portia inflicts on all her suitors, from preexisting sources. *The Merchant of Venice*'s Italian setting and marriage plot are typical of Shakespeare's earlier comedies, but the characters of Portia, Shakespeare's first great heroine, and the unforgettable villain Shylock elevate this play to a new level.

Shylock's cries for a pound of flesh have made him one of literature's most memorable villains, but many readers and playgoers have found him a compelling and sympathetic figure. The question of whether or not Shakespeare endorses the anti-Semitism of the Christian characters in the play has been much debated. Jews in Shakespeare's England were a marginalized group, and Shakespeare's contemporaries would have been very familiar with portrayals of Jews as villains and objects of mockery. For example, Christopher Marlowe's *The Jew of Malta,* a bloody farce about a murderous Jewish villain, was a great popular success and would have been fresh in Shakespeare's mind as he set about creating his own Jewish character. Shakespeare certainly draws on this anti-Semitic tradition in portraying Shylock, exploiting Jewish stereotypes for comic effect. But Shylock is a more complex character than the Jew in Marlowe's play, and Shakespeare makes him seem more human by showing that his hatred is born of the mistreatment he has suffered in a Christian society. Shakespeare's character includes an element of pathos as well as comedy, meaning that he elicits from readers and audiences pity and compassion, rather than simply scorn and derision.

Plot Overview

ANTONIO, A VENETIAN MERCHANT, complains to his friends of a melancholy that he cannot explain. His friend Bassanio is desperately in need of money to court Portia, a wealthy heiress who lives in the city of Belmont. Bassanio asks Antonio for a loan in order to travel in style to Portia's estate. Antonio agrees, but is unable to make the loan himself because his own money is all invested in a number of trade ships that are still at sea. Antonio suggests that Bassanio secure the loan from one of the city's moneylenders and name Antonio as the loan's guarantor. In Belmont, Portia expresses sadness over the terms of her father's will, which stipulates that she must marry the man who correctly chooses one of three caskets. None of Portia's current suitors are to her liking, and she and her lady-in-waiting, Nerissa, fondly remember a visit paid some time before by Bassanio.

In Venice, Antonio and Bassanio approach Shylock, a Jewish moneylender, for a loan. Shylock nurses a long-standing grudge against Antonio, who has made a habit of berating Shylock and other Jews for their usury, the practice of loaning money at exorbitant rates of interest, and who undermines their business by offering interest-free loans. Although Antonio refuses to apologize for his behavior, Shylock acts agreeably and offers to lend Bassanio three thousand ducats with no interest. Shylock adds, however, that should the loan go unpaid, Shylock will be entitled to a pound of Antonio's own flesh. Despite Bassanio's warnings, Antonio agrees. In Shylock's own household, his servant Launcelot decides to leave Shylock's service to work for Bassanio, and Shylock's daughter Jessica schemes to elope with Antonio's friend Lorenzo. That night, the streets of Venice fill up with revelers, and Jessica escapes with Lorenzo by dressing as his page. After a night of celebration, Bassanio and his friend Gratiano leave for Belmont, where Bassanio intends to win Portia's hand.

In Belmont, Portia welcomes the prince of Morocco, who has come in an attempt to choose the right casket to marry her. The prince studies the inscriptions on the three caskets and chooses the gold one, which proves to be an incorrect choice. In Venice, Shylock is furious to find that his daughter has run away, but rejoices in the fact that Antonio's ships are rumored to have been wrecked and that he will soon be able to claim his debt. In Belmont, the prince of Arragon also visits Portia. He, too, studies the caskets carefully, but he picks the silver one, which is also incorrect. Bassanio arrives at Portia's estate, and they declare their love for one another. Despite Portia's request that he wait before choosing, Bassanio immediately picks the correct casket, which is made of lead. He and Portia rejoice, and Gratiano confesses that he has fallen in love with Nerissa. The couples decide on a double wedding. Portia gives Bassanio a ring as a token of love, and makes him swear that under no circumstances will he part with it. They are joined, unexpectedly, by Lorenzo and Jessica. The celebration, however, is cut short by the news that Antonio has indeed lost his ships, and that he has forfeited his bond to Shylock. Bassanio and Gratiano immediately travel to Venice to try and save Antonio's life. After they leave, Portia tells Nerissa that they will go to Venice disguised as men.

Shylock ignores the many pleas to spare Antonio's life, and a trial is called to decide the matter. The duke of Venice, who presides over the trial, announces that he has sent for a legal expert, who turns out to be Portia disguised as a young man of law. Portia asks Shylock to show mercy, but he remains inflexible and insists the pound of flesh is rightfully his. Bassanio offers Shylock twice the money due him, but Shylock insists on collecting the bond as it is written. Portia examines the contract and, finding it legally binding, declares that Shylock is entitled to the merchant's flesh. Shylock ecstatically praises her wisdom, but as he is on the verge of collecting his due, Portia reminds him that he must do so without causing Antonio to bleed, as the contract does not entitle him to any blood. Trapped by this logic, Shylock hastily agrees to take Bassanio's money instead, but Portia insists that Shylock take his bond as written, or nothing at all. Portia informs Shylock that he is guilty of conspiring against the life of a Venetian citizen, which means he must turn over half of his property to the state and the other half to Antonio. The duke spares Shylock's life and takes a fine instead of Shylock's property. Antonio also forgoes his half of Shylock's wealth on two conditions: first, Shylock must convert to Christianity, and second, he must will the entirety of his estate to Lorenzo and Jessica upon his death. Shylock agrees and takes his leave.

Bassanio, who does not see through Portia's disguise, showers the young law clerk with thanks, and is eventually pressured into giving Portia the ring with which he promised never to part. Gratiano gives

Nerissa, who is disguised as Portia's clerk, his ring. The two women return to Belmont, where they find Lorenzo and Jessica declaring their love to each other under the moonlight. When Bassanio and Gratiano arrive the next day, their wives accuse them of faithlessly giving their rings to other women. Before the deception goes too far, however, Portia reveals that she was, in fact, the law clerk, and both she and Nerissa reconcile with their husbands. Lorenzo and Jessica are pleased to learn of their inheritance from Shylock, and the joyful news arrives that Antonio's ships have in fact made it back safely. The group celebrates its good fortune.

CHARACTER LIST

Shylock   A Jewish moneylender in Venice. Angered by his mistreatment at the hands of Venice's Christians, particularly Antonio, Shylock schemes to eke out his revenge by ruthlessly demanding as payment a pound of Antonio's flesh. Although seen by the rest of the play's characters as an inhuman monster, Shylock at times diverges from stereotype and reveals himself to be quite human. These contradictions, and his eloquent expressions of hatred, have earned Shylock a place as one of Shakespeare's most memorable characters.

Portia   A wealthy heiress from Belmont. Portia's beauty is matched only by her intelligence. Bound by a clause in her father's will that forces her to marry whichever suitor chooses correctly among three caskets, Portia is nonetheless able to marry her true love, Bassanio. Far and away the most clever of the play's characters, it is Portia, in the disguise of a young law clerk, who saves Antonio from Shylock's knife.

Antonio   The merchant whose love for his friend Bassanio prompts him to sign Shylock's contract and almost lose his life. Antonio is something of a mercurial figure, often inexplicably melancholy and, as Shylock points out, possessed of an incorrigible dislike of Jews. Nonetheless, Antonio is beloved of his friends and proves merciful to Shylock, albeit with conditions.

Bassanio   A gentleman of Venice, and a kinsman and dear friend to Antonio. Bassanio's love for the wealthy Portia leads him to borrow money from Shylock with Antonio as his guarantor. An ineffectual businessman, Bassanio proves himself a worthy suitor, correctly identifying the casket that contains Portia's portrait.

Gratiano   A friend of Bassanio's who accompanies him to Belmont. A coarse and garrulous young man, Gratiano is Shylock's most vocal and insulting critic during the trial. While Bassanio courts Portia, Gratiano falls in love with and eventually weds Portia's lady-in-waiting, Nerissa.

Jessica   Although she is Shylock's daughter, Jessica hates life in her father's house, and elopes with the young Christian gentleman, Lorenzo. The fate of her soul is often in doubt: the play's characters wonder if her marriage can overcome the fact that she was born a Jew, and we wonder if her sale of a ring given to her father by her mother is excessively callous.

Lorenzo   A friend of Bassanio and Antonio, Lorenzo is in love with Shylock's daughter, Jessica. He schemes to help Jessica escape from her father's house, and he eventually elopes with her to Belmont.

Nerissa   Portia's lady-in-waiting and confidante. She marries Gratiano and escorts Portia on Portia's trip to Venice by disguising herself as her law clerk.

Launcelot Gobbo   Bassanio's servant. A comical, clownish figure who is especially adept at making puns, Launcelot leaves Shylock's service in order to work for Bassanio.

The prince of Morocco   A Moorish prince who seeks Portia's hand in marriage. The prince of Morocco asks Portia to ignore his dark countenance and seeks to win her by picking one of the three caskets. Certain that the caskets reflect Portia's beauty and stature, the prince of Morocco picks the gold chest, which proves to be incorrect.

The prince of Arragon   An arrogant Spanish nobleman who also attempts to win Portia's hand by picking a casket. Like the prince of Morocco, however, the prince of Arragon chooses unwisely. He picks the silver casket, which gives him a message calling him an idiot instead of Portia's hand.

Salarino   A Venetian gentleman, and friend to Antonio, Bassanio, and Lorenzo. Salarino escorts the newlyweds Jessica and Lorenzo to Belmont, and returns with Bassanio and Gratiano for Antonio's trial. He is often almost indistinguishable from his companion Solanio.

Solanio   A Venetian gentleman, and frequent counterpart to Salarino.

The duke of Venice   The ruler of Venice, who presides over Antonio's trial. Although a powerful man, the duke's state is built on respect for the law, and he is unable to help Antonio.

Old Gobbo   Launcelot's father, also a servant in Venice.

Tubal   A Jew in Venice, and one of Shylock's friends.

Doctor Bellario   A wealthy Paduan lawyer and Portia's cousin. Doctor Bellario never appears in the play, but he gives Portia's servant the letters of introduction needed for her to make her appearance in court.

Balthasar   Portia's servant, whom she dispatches to get the appropriate materials from Doctor Bellario.

ANALYSIS OF MAJOR CHARACTERS

SHYLOCK

Although critics tend to agree that Shylock is *The Merchant of Venice*'s most noteworthy figure, no consensus has been reached on whether to read him as a bloodthirsty bogeyman, a clownish Jewish stereotype, or a tragic figure whose sense of decency has been fractured by the persecution he endures. Certainly, Shylock is the play's antagonist, and he is menacing enough to seriously imperil the happiness of Venice's businessmen and young lovers alike. Shylock is also, however, a creation of circumstance; even in his single-minded pursuit of a pound of flesh, his frequent mentions of the cruelty he has endured at Christian hands make it hard for us to label him a natural born monster. In one of Shakespeare's most famous monologues, for example, Shylock argues that Jews are humans and calls his quest for vengeance the product of lessons taught to him by the cruelty of Venetian citizens. On the other hand, Shylock's coldly calculated attempt to revenge the wrongs done to him by murdering his persecutor, Antonio, prevents us from viewing him in a primarily positive light. Shakespeare gives us unmistakably human moments, but he often steers us against Shylock as well, painting him as a miserly, cruel, and prosaic figure.

PORTIA

Quick-witted, wealthy, and beautiful, Portia embodies the virtues that are typical of Shakespeare's heroines—it is no surprise that she emerges as the antidote to Shylock's malice. At the beginning of the play, however, we do not see Portia's potential for initiative and resourcefulness, as she is a near prisoner, feeling herself absolutely bound to follow her father's dying wishes. This opening appearance, however, proves to be a revealing introduction to Portia, who emerges as that rarest of combinations—a free spirit who abides rigidly by rules. Rather than ignoring the stipulations of her father's will, she watches a stream of suitors pass her by, happy to see these particular suitors go, but sad that she has no choice in the matter. When Bassanio arrives, however, Portia proves herself to be highly resourceful, begging the man she loves to stay a while before picking a chest, and finding loopholes in the will's provision that we never thought possible. Also, in her defeat of Shylock Portia prevails by applying a more rigid standard than Shylock himself, agreeing that his contract very much entitles him to his pound of flesh, but adding that it does not allow for any loss of blood. Anybody can break the rules, but Portia's effectiveness comes from her ability to make the law work for her.

Portia rejects the stuffiness that rigid adherence to the law might otherwise suggest. In her courtroom appearance, she vigorously applies the law, but still flouts convention by appearing disguised as a man. After depriving Bassanio of his ring, she stops the prank before it goes to far, but still takes it far enough to berate Bassanio and Gratiano for their callousness, and she even insinuates that she has been unfaithful.

ANTONIO

Although the play's title refers to him, Antonio is a rather lackluster character. He emerges in Act I, scene i as a hopeless depressive, someone who cannot name the source of his melancholy and who, throughout the course of the play, devolves into a self-pitying lump, unable to muster the energy required to defend himself against execution. Antonio never names the cause of his melancholy, but the evidence seems to point to his being in love, despite his denial of this idea in Act I, scene i. The most likely object of his affection is Bassanio, who takes full advantage of the merchant's boundless feelings for him. Antonio has risked the entirety of his fortune on overseas trading ventures, yet he agrees to guarantee the potentially lethal loan Bassanio secures from Shylock. In the context of his unrequited and presumably unconsummated relationship with Bassanio, Antonio's willingness to offer up a pound of his own flesh seems particularly important, signifying a union that grotesquely alludes to the rites of marriage, where two partners become "one flesh."

Further evidence of the nature of Antonio's feelings for Bassanio appears later in the play, when Antonio's proclamations resonate with the hyperbole and self-satisfaction of a doomed lover's declaration: "Pray God Bassanio come / To see me pay his debt, and then I care not" (III.iii.35–36). Antonio ends the play as happily as he can, restored to wealth even if not delivered into love. Without a mate, he is indeed the "tainted wether"—or castrated ram—of the flock, and he will likely return to his favorite pastime of moping about the streets of Venice (IV.i.113). After all, he has effectively disabled himself from pursuing his other hobby—abusing Shylock—by insisting that the Jew convert to Christianity. Although a sixteenth-century audience might have seen this demand as merciful, as Shylock is saving himself from eternal damnation by converting, we are less likely to be convinced. Not only does Antonio's reputation as an anti-Semite precede him, but the only instance in the play when he breaks out of his doldrums is his "storm" against Shylock (I.iii.132). In this context, Antonio proves that the dominant threads of his character are melancholy and cruelty.

Themes, Motifs & Symbols

Themes

Themes are the fundamental and often universal ideas explored in a literary work.

SELF-INTEREST VERSUS LOVE

On the surface, the main difference between the Christian characters and Shylock appears to be that the Christian characters value human relationships over business ones, whereas Shylock is only interested in money. The Christian characters certainly view the matter this way. Merchants like Antonio lend money free of interest and put themselves at risk for those they love, whereas Shylock agonizes over the loss of his money and is reported to run through the streets crying, "O, my ducats! O, my daughter!" (II.viii.15). With these words, he apparently values his money at least as much as his daughter, suggesting that his greed outweighs his love. However, upon closer inspection, this supposed difference between Christian and Jew breaks down. When we see Shylock in Act III, scene i, he seems more hurt by the fact that his daughter sold a ring that was given to him by his dead wife before they were married than he is by the loss of the ring's monetary value. Some human relationships do indeed matter to Shylock more than money. Moreover, his insistence that he have a pound of flesh rather than any amount of money shows that his resentment is much stronger than his greed.

Just as Shylock's character seems hard to pin down, the Christian characters also present an inconsistent picture. Though Portia and Bassanio come to love one another, Bassanio seeks her hand in the first place because he is monstrously in debt and needs her money. Bassanio even asks Antonio to look at the money he lends Bassanio as an investment, though Antonio insists that he lends him the money solely out of love. In other words, Bassanio is anxious to view his relationship with Antonio as a matter of business rather than of love. Finally, Shylock eloquently argues that Jews are human beings just as Christians are, but Christians such as Antonio hate Jews simply because they are Jews. Thus, while the Christian characters may talk more about mercy, love, and charity, they are not always consistent in how they display these qualities.

THE DIVINE QUALITY OF MERCY

The conflict between Shylock and the Christian characters comes to a head over the issue of mercy. The other characters acknowledge that the law is on Shylock's side, but they all expect him to show mercy, which he refuses to do. When, during the trial, Shylock asks Portia what could possibly compel him to be merciful, Portia's long reply, beginning with the words, "The quality of mercy is not strained," clarifies what is at stake in the argument (IV.i.179). Human beings should be merciful because God is merciful: mercy is an attribute of God himself and therefore greater than power, majesty, or law. Portia's understanding of mercy is based on the way Christians in Shakespeare's time understood the difference between the Old and New Testaments. According to the writings of St. Paul in the New Testament, the Old Testament depicts God as requiring strict adherence to rules and exacting harsh punishments for those who stray. The New Testament, in contrast, emphasizes adherence to the spirit rather than the letter of the law, portraying a God who forgives rather than punishes and offers salvation to those followers who forgive others. Thus, when Portia warns Shylock against pursuing the law without regard for mercy, she is promoting what Elizabethan Christians would have seen as a pro-Christian, anti-Jewish agenda.

The strictures of Renaissance drama demanded that Shylock be a villain, and, as such, patently unable to show even a drop of compassion for his enemy. A sixteenth-century audience would not expect Shylock to exercise mercy—therefore, it is up to the Christians to do so. Once she has turned Shylock's greatest weapon—the law—against him, Portia has the opportunity to give freely of the mercy for which she so beautifully advocates. Instead, she backs Shylock into a corner, where she strips him of his bond, his estate, and his dignity, forcing him to kneel and beg for mercy. Given that Antonio decides not to seize Shylock's goods as punishment for conspiring against him, we might consider Antonio to be merciful. But we may also question whether it is merciful to return to Shylock half of his goods, only to take away his religion and his profession. By forcing Shylock to convert, Antonio disables him from practicing usury, which, according to Shylock's reports, was Antonio's primary reason for berating and spitting on him in public. Antonio's compassion, then, seems to stem as much from self-interest as from concern for his fellow man. Mercy, as delivered in *The Merchant of Venice*, never manages to be as sweet, selfless, or full of grace as Portia presents it.

HATRED AS A CYCLICAL PHENOMENON

Throughout the play, Shylock claims that he is simply applying the lessons taught to him by his Christian neighbors; this claim becomes an integral part of both his character and his argument in court. In Shylock's very first appearance, as he conspires to harm Antonio, his entire plan seems to be born of the insults and injuries Antonio has inflicted upon him in the past. As the play continues, and Shylock unveils more of his reasoning, the same idea rears its head over and over—he is simply applying what years of abuse have taught him. Responding to Salarino's query of what good the pound of flesh will do him, Shylock responds, "The villainy you teach me I will execute, and it shall go hard but I will better the instruction" (III.i.60–61). Not all of Shylock's actions can be blamed on poor teachings, and one could argue that Antonio understands his own culpability in his near execution. With the trial's conclusion, Antonio demands that Shylock convert to Christianity, but inflicts no other punishment, despite the threats of fellow Christians like Gratiano. Antonio does not, as he has in the past, kick or spit on Shylock. Antonio, as well as the duke, effectively ends the conflict by starving it of the injustices it needs to continue.

MOTIFS

Motifs are recurring structures, contrasts, and literary devices that can help to develop and inform the text's major themes.

THE LAW

The Merchant of Venice depends heavily upon laws and rules—the laws of the state of Venice and the rules stipulated in contracts and wills. Laws and rules can be manipulated for cruel or wanton purposes, but they are also capable of producing good when executed by the right people. Portia's virtual imprisonment by the game of caskets seems, at first, like a questionable rule at best, but her likening of the game to a lottery system is belied by the fact that, in the end, it works perfectly. The game keeps a host of suitors at bay, and of the three who try to choose the correct casket to win Portia's hand, only the man of Portia's desires succeeds. By the time Bassanio picks the correct chest, the choice seems like a more efficient indicator of human nature than any person could ever provide. A similar phenomenon occurs with Venetian law. Until Portia's arrival, Shylock is the law's strictest adherent, and it seems as if the city's adherence to contracts will result in tragedy. However, when Portia arrives and manipulates the law most skillfully of all, the outcome is the happiest ending of all, at least to an Elizabethan audience: Antonio is rescued and Shylock forced to abandon his religion. The fact that the trial is such a close call does, however, raise the fearful specter of how the law can be misused. Without the proper guidance, the law can be wielded to do horrible things.

CROSS-DRESSING

Twice in the play, daring escapes are executed with the help of cross-dressing. Jessica escapes the tedium of Shylock's house by dressing as a page, while Portia and Nerissa rescue Antonio by posing as officers of the Venetian court. This device was not only familiar to Renaissance drama, but essential to its performance: women were banned from the stage and their parts were performed by prepubescent boys. Shakespeare was a great fan of the potentials of cross-dressing and used the device often, especially in his comedies. But Portia reveals that the donning of men's clothes is more than mere comedy. She says that she has studied a "thousand raw tricks of these bragging Jacks," implying that male authority is a kind of performance that can be imitated successfully (III.iv.77). She feels confident that she can outwit any male competitor, declaring, "I'll prove the prettier fellow of the two, / And wear my dagger with the braver grace" (III.iv.64–65). In short, by assuming the clothes of the opposite sex, Portia enables herself to assume the power and position denied to her as a woman.

FILIAL PIETY

Like Shakespeare's other comedies, *The Merchant of Venice* seems to endorse the behavior of characters who treat filial piety lightly, even though the heroine, Portia, sets the opposite example by obeying her father's will. Launcelot greets his blind, long lost father by giving the old man confusing directions and telling the old man that his beloved son Launcelot is dead. This moment of impertinence can be excused as essential to the comedy of the play, but it sets the stage for Jessica's far more complex hatred of her father. Jessica can list no specific complaints when she explains her desire to leave Shylock's house, and in the one scene in which she appears with

Shylock, he fusses over her in a way that some might see as tender. Jessica's desire to leave is made clearer when the other characters note how separate she has become from her father, but her behavior after departing seems questionable at best. Most notably, she trades her father's ring, given to him by her dead mother, for a monkey. The frivolity of this exchange, in which an heirloom is tossed away for the silliest of objects, makes for quite a disturbing image of the esteem in which *The Merchant of Venice*'s children hold their parents, and puts us, at least temporarily, in Shylock's corner.

SYMBOLS

Symbols are objects, characters, figures, and colors used to represent abstract ideas or concepts.

THE THREE CASKETS

The contest for Portia's hand, in which suitors from various countries choose among a gold, a silver, and a lead casket, resembles the cultural and legal system of Venice in some respects. Like the Venice of the play, the casket contest presents the same opportunities and the same rules to men of various nations, ethnicities, and religions. Also like Venice, the hidden bias of the casket test is fundamentally Christian. To win Portia, Bassanio must ignore the gold casket, which bears the inscription, "Who chooseth me shall gain what many men desire" (II.vii.5), and the silver casket, which says, "Who chooseth me shall get as much as he deserves" (II.vii.7). The correct casket is lead and warns that the person who chooses it must give and risk everything he has. The contest combines a number of Christian teachings, such as the idea that desire is an unreliable guide and should be resisted, and the idea that human beings do not deserve God's grace but receive it in spite of themselves. Christianity teaches that appearances are often deceiving, and that people should not trust the evidence provided by the senses—hence the humble appearance of the lead casket. Faith and charity are the central values of Christianity, and these values are evoked by the lead casket's injunction to give all and risk all, as one does in making a leap of faith. Portia's father has presented marriage as one in which the proper suitor risks and gives everything for the spouse, in the hope of a divine recompense he can never truly deserve. The contest certainly suits Bassanio, who knows he does not deserve his good fortune but is willing to risk everything on a gamble.

SYMBOLS

THE POUND OF FLESH

The pound of flesh that Shylock seeks lends itself to multiple interpretations: it emerges most as a metaphor for two of the play's closest relationships, but also calls attention to Shylock's inflexible adherence to the law. The fact that Bassanio's debt is to be paid with Antonio's flesh is significant, showing how their friendship is so binding it has made them almost one. Shylock's determination is strengthened by Jessica's departure, as if he were seeking recompense for the loss of his own flesh and blood by collecting it from his enemy. Lastly, the pound of flesh is a constant reminder of the rigidity of Shylock's world, where numerical calculations are used to evaluate even the most serious of situations. Shylock never explicitly demands that Antonio die, but asks instead, in his numerical mind, for a pound in exchange for his three thousand ducats. Where the other characters measure their emotions with long metaphors and words, Shylock measures everything in far more prosaic and numerical quantities.

LEAH'S RING

The ring given to Shylock in his bachelor days by a woman named Leah, who is most likely Shylock's wife and Jessica's mother, gets only a brief mention in the play, but is still an object of great importance. When told that Jessica has stolen it and traded it for a monkey, Shylock very poignantly laments its loss: "I would not have given it for a wilderness of monkeys" (III.i.101–102). The lost ring allows us to see Shylock in an uncharacteristically vulnerable position and to view him as a human being capable of feeling something more than anger. Although Shylock and Tubal discuss the ring for no more than five lines, the ring stands as an important symbol of Shylock's humanity, his ability to love, and his ability to grieve.

Summary & Analysis

Act I, scenes i–ii

Summary: Act I, scene i

Antonio, a Venetian merchant, complains to his friends, Salarino and Solanio, that a sadness has overtaken him and dulled his faculties, although he is at a loss to explain why. Salarino and Solanio suggest that his sadness must be due to his commercial investments, for Antonio has dispatched several trade ships to various ports. Salarino says it is impossible for Antonio not to feel sad at the thought of the perilous ocean sinking his entire investment, but Antonio assures his friends that his business ventures do not depend on the safe passage of any one ship. Solanio then declares that Antonio must be in love, but Antonio dismisses the suggestion.

The three men encounter Bassanio, Antonio's kinsman, walking with two friends named Lorenzo and Gratiano. Salarino and Solanio bid Antonio farewell and depart. When Gratiano notices Antonio's unhappiness and suggests that the merchant worries too much about business, Antonio responds that he is but a player on a stage, destined to play a sad part. Gratiano warns Antonio against becoming the type of man who affects a solemn demeanor in order to gain a wise reputation, then he takes his leave with Lorenzo. Bassanio jokes that Gratiano has terribly little to say, claiming that his friend's wise remarks prove as elusive as "two grains of wheat hid in two bushels of chaff" (I.i.115–116). Antonio asks Bassanio to tell him about the clandestine love that Bassanio is harboring. In reply, Bassanio admits that although he already owes Antonio a substantial sum of money from his earlier, more extravagant days, he has fallen in love with Portia, a rich heiress from Belmont, and hopes to win her heart by holding his own with her other wealthy and powerful suitors. In order to woo Portia, however, Bassanio says he needs to borrow more money from Antonio. Antonio replies that he cannot give Bassanio another loan, as all his money is tied up in his present business ventures, but offers to guarantee any loan Bassanio can round up.

SUMMARY: ACT I, SCENE II

At Belmont, Portia complains to her lady-in-waiting, Nerissa, that she is weary of the world because, as her dead father's will stipulates, she cannot decide for herself whether to take a husband. Instead, Portia's various suitors must choose between three chests, one of gold, one of silver, and one of lead, in the hopes of selecting the one that contains her portrait. The man who guesses correctly will win Portia's hand in marriage, but those who guess incorrectly must swear never to marry anyone. Nerissa lists the suitors who have come to guess—a Neapolitan prince, a Palatine count, a French nobleman, an English baron, a Scottish lord, and the nephew of the duke of Saxony—and Portia criticizes their many hilarious faults. For instance, she describes the Neapolitan prince as being too fond of his horse, the Palatine count as being too serious, the Englishman as lacking any knowledge of Italian or any of the other languages Portia speaks, and the German suitor of drunkenness. Each of these suitors has left without even attempting a guess for fear of the penalty for guessing wrong. This fact relieves Portia, and both she and Nerissa remember Bassanio, who has visited once before, as the suitor most deserving and worthy of praise. A servant enters to tell Portia that the prince of Morocco will arrive soon, news that Portia is not at all happy to hear.

ANALYSIS: ACT I, SCENES I–II

The first scene of the play introduces us to a world of wealthy, upper-class Christian men living in Venice. Their conversation reveals that they are men of business who take great risks with money and are careful to avoid seeming overly concerned about their investments. For example, Antonio calmly denies his associates' suggestion that he is worried about his ships, and Salarino's description of a shipwreck, with silks enrobing the roaring waters and spices scattered upon the stream, is lyrical and poetic rather than practical or business-minded. Significantly, the conversation throughout this opening scene is not really about business, but rather Antonio's emotional state—his friends see it as their duty to cheer him up. We may infer that money is very important to these men, but the code of manners that they share requires them to act as though friendship, camaraderie, and good cheer matter more than money. For example, Salarino excuses himself by asserting that his only concern is to make Antonio merry and that he is leaving because better friends have arrived, but Antonio knows that Salarino is leaving to attend to his own business affairs. The Christian men of the play share a certain set of values, but these values are not always entirely consistent or self-evident.

However, if the professions of affection between Antonio and the other merchants simply seem like good manners, Antonio's loyalty toward his friend Bassanio is obviously quite sincere. Where Bassanio is concerned, love and friendship really are more important to Antonio than money. When Bassanio asks for help, Antonio promptly offers all of his money and credit, insisting that they go straightaway to a lender so he can stand as security for Bassanio. Antonio's defining characteristic is his willingness to do anything for his friend Bassanio, even lay down his life. Beyond this willingness to sacrifice himself for Bassanio, Antonio is a relatively passive character. He begins the play in a dreamy melancholy that he does not know how to cure, and throughout the play he never takes decisive action in the way that Bassanio, Portia, and various other characters do. He approaches life with a pensive, resigned, wait-and-see attitude, like a merchant waiting for his ships to return.

One possible explanation for Antonio's melancholy is that he is hopelessly in love with Bassanio. Although he never admits it, the evidence suggests that he is in love with *somebody*. His friends think he is in love, and while he denies the suggestion that he is worried about his ships with a calm, well-reasoned argument, he responds to the suggestion that he is in love with a simple "[f]ie, fie" (I.i.46). Moreover, melancholy was traditionally regarded as a symptom of lovesickness in Shakespeare's time, yet no female lover for Antonio is alluded to in the play. Antonio is extravagant in his professions of love for Bassanio, and while extravagant protestations of love between upper-class men were not considered abnormal at the time, we may hear a double entendre in his assurance that "[m]y purse, my person, my extremest means / Lie all unlocked to your occasions" (I.i.138–139). The explicit sense of this statement is that Antonio will make himself and his physical person available to help Bassanio, but it could be construed to mean that his body, or person, is available for Bassanio's pleasure. The idea that Antonio is in love with Bassanio would explain his motivation for risking his life, as well as lend his character a certain poignancy, as Antonio puts his own life and wealth in jeopardy to help Bassanio woo someone else.

Act I, scene ii introduces Portia, the heroine of the play, and establishes the casket test through which she will find a husband. After we see more of Portia, her compliance with her dead father's instructions may seem odd, as she proves to be an extremely independent and strong-willed character. However, her adherence to her father's will establishes an important aspect of her character: she plays by the rules. Her strict adherence to laws and other strictures makes her an interesting counterpoint to Shylock, the play's villain, whom we meet in the next scene.

Because Portia is such a fabulously wealthy heiress, the only men eligible to court her are from the highest end of the social strata. As a result, the competition between her suitors is international, including noblemen from various parts of Europe and even Africa. Portia's description of her previous suitors serves as a vehicle for Shakespeare to satirize the nobleman of France, Scotland, Germany, and England for the amusement of his English audience. At the end of the scene, the arrival of the prince of Morocco is announced, introducing a suitor who is racially and culturally more distant from Portia than her previous suitors. The casket test seems designed to give an equal chance to all of these different noblemen, so the competition for Portia's hand and wealth in Belmont parallels the financial community of Venice, which is also organized to include men of many nations, Christian and non-Christian alike. Portia's remarks about the prince of Morocco's devilish skin color, however, show that she is rooting for a husband who is culturally and racially similar to her. In fact, she hopes to marry Bassanio, the suitor with the background closest to hers.

ACT I, SCENE III

SUMMARY

Shylock, a Jewish moneylender, agrees to loan Bassanio three thousand ducats for a term of three months. Bassanio assures Shylock that Antonio will guarantee the loan, but Shylock is doubtful because Antonio's wealth is currently invested in business ventures that may fail. In the end, however, Shylock decides that Antonio's guarantee of the loan will be sufficient assurance, and asks to speak with him. When Antonio arrives, Shylock, in an aside, confesses his hatred for the man. Antonio, Shylock says, is a Christian who lends money without interest, which makes more difficult the practice of usury, in which money is lent out at exorbitant interest rates. Shylock is also incensed by Antonio's frequent public denunciations of Shylock. Antonio makes it clear to Shylock that he is not in the habit of borrowing or lending money, but has decided to make an exception on behalf of his friend Bassanio. Their conversation leads Antonio to chastise the business of usury, which Shylock defends as a way to thrive.

As he calculates the interest on Bassanio's loan, Shylock remembers the many times that Antonio has cursed him, calling him a "misbeliever, cut-throat, dog / And spit upon [his] Jewish gaberdine" (I.iii.107–108). Antonio responds that he is likely to do so again, and insists that Shylock lend him the money as an enemy. Such an arrangement, Antonio claims, will make it easier for Shylock to exact a harsh penalty if the loan is not repaid. Assuring Antonio that he means to be friends, Shylock offers to make the loan without interest. Instead, he suggests, seemingly in jest, that Antonio forfeit a pound of his own flesh should the loan not be repaid in due time. Bassanio warns Antonio against entering such an agreement, but Antonio assures him that he will have no trouble repaying the debt, as his ships will soon bring him wealth that far exceeds the value of the loan. Shylock attempts to dismiss Bassanio's suspicions, asking what profit he stands to make by procuring a pound of Antonio's flesh. As Shylock heads off to the notary's office to sign the bond, Antonio remarks on Shylock's newfound generosity: "The Hebrew will turn Christian; he grows kind" (I.iii.174). Bassanio remains suspicious of the arrangement, but Antonio reminds him that his ships will arrive within the next two months.

ANALYSIS

Shylock is an arresting presence on the stage, and although Antonio may be the character for whom the play is named, it is Shylock who has come to dominate the imaginations of critics and audiences alike. Shylock's physical presence in the play is actually not so large, as he speaks fewer lines than other characters and does not even appear in the play's final act. However, in many ways, the play belongs to Shylock. The use of a Jew as the central villain was not unknown to Renaissance comedy, as evidenced by *The Jew of Malta,* a wildly popular play by Shakespeare's contemporary Christopher Marlowe, which revolves around a malevolent, bloodthirsty Jewish character named Barabas. Shylock, however, differs in that his malice seems to stem, at least in part, from the unkindness of his Christian colleagues. Exactly how to read Shylock has been a matter of some debate, and even the most persuasive scholars would be hard-pressed to call him a flattering portrait of a Jew. One could certainly argue, however, that Shylock receives far less of a stock portrayal than what was common in Shakespeare's time, and that, given the constant degradation he endures, we can even feel something akin to sympathy for him.

At the heart of any sympathy we might feel for Shylock lies the fact that the bonhomie and good nature that so mark Antonio's appearance with Bassanio disappear, and his treatment of Shylock is unexpectedly harsh and brutal. Even though Bassanio and Antonio require a favor from Shylock, Antonio's is still a tone of imperious command, and his past, present, and future attitude toward Shylock is one of exceptional contempt. Shylock vividly illustrates the depth of this contempt, wondering aloud why he should lend Antonio money when Antonio has voided his "rheum," or spit, on Shylock's beard, and he kicked Shylock as he would a stray dog (I.iii.113–114). The repeated mention of spittle here sharply differentiates Antonio's Venice, where even shipwrecks seem like spice-laden dreams, from Shylock's, where the city is a place of blows, kicks, and bodily functions. Without these details, Antonio's haughty attitude toward Shylock could easily be forgiven, but the very visceral details of spit and kicks show a violent, less romantic side to Antonio, and our sympathies for him cannot help but lessen.

Shylock is noticeably different from Shakespeare's other great villains, such as Richard III or Iago, in several ways. In the first place, these other villains see themselves as evil, and while they may try to justify their own villainy, they also revel in it, making asides to the audience and self-consciously comparing themselves to the Vice character of medieval morality plays. Marlowe's Jew, Barabas, is a similarly self-conscious villain. Though the Christian characters of *The Merchant of Venice* may view Jews as evil, Shylock does not see himself in that way. His views of himself and others are rational, articulate, and consistent. Also, Shakespeare's other villains are generally more deceitful, passing themselves off as loving and virtuous Christians while plotting malevolently against those around them. Shylock, on the other hand, is an outcast even before the play begins, vilified and spat upon by the Christian characters. Shylock's actions are relatively open, although the other characters misunderstand his intentions because they do not understand him.

Indeed, Shylock understands the Christians and their culture much better than they understand him. The Christian characters only interact with Shylock within a framework of finance and law—he is not part of the friendship network portrayed in Act I, scene i. Though Bassanio asks him to dine with them, Shylock says in an aside that he will not break bread with Christians, nor will he forgive Antonio, thereby signaling his rejection of one of the fundamental Christian values, forgiveness. Shylock is able to cite the New Testament as readily as Jewish scripture, as he shows in his remark about the pig being the animal into which Christ drove the devil. Antonio notes Shylock's facility with the Bible, but he uses this ability to compare Shylock to the devil, who, proverbially, is also adept at quoting scripture. As we see more of Shylock, he does not become a hero or a fully sympathetic character, but he is an unsettling figure insofar as he exposes the inconsistencies and hypocrisies of the Christian characters. Shylock never quite fits their descriptions or expectations of him. Most significantly, they think he is motivated solely by money, when in fact his resentment against Antonio and the other Christians outweighs his desire for monetary gain.

ACT II, SCENES I–IV

SUMMARY: ACT II, SCENE I
In Belmont, the prince of Morocco arrives to attempt to win Portia's hand in marriage. The prince asks Portia not to judge him by his dark complexion, assuring her that he is as valorous as any European man. Portia reminds the prince that her own tastes do not matter, since the process of picking chests, stipulated in her father's will, makes the prince as worthy as any other suitor. With a lengthy proclamation of his own bravery and heroism, the prince asks Portia to lead him to the caskets, where he may venture his guess. She reminds him that the penalty for guessing incorrectly is that he must remain unmarried forever. The prince accepts this stipulation, and Portia leads him off to dinner.

SUMMARY: ACT II, SCENE II
Launcelot Gobbo, a servant of Shylock's, struggles to decide whether or not he should run away from his master. Part of him, which he calls "[t]he fiend . . . at mine elbow," wants to leave, while his conscience reminds him of his honest nature and urges him to stay (II.ii.2). Although Launcelot has no specific complaints, he seems troubled by the fact that his master is Jewish, or, as Launcelot puts it, "a kind of devil" (II.ii.19). Just when Launcelot determines to run away, his father, Old Gobbo, enters. The old man is blind, and he asks how to get to Shylock's house, where he hopes to find young Launcelot. Because his father does not recognize him, Launcelot decides to play a prank on him—he gives the old man confusing directions and

reports that Launcelot is dead. When Launcelot reveals the deception, Old Gobbo doubts that the man before him is his son, but Launcelot soon convinces his father of his identity. Launcelot confesses to his father that he is leaving Shylock's employment in the hopes of serving Bassanio. Just then, Bassanio enters and the two plead with him to accept Launcelot as his servant. Bassanio takes several moments to understand their bumbling proposition, but he accepts the offer. Bassanio then meets Gratiano, who asks to accompany him to Belmont, and agrees on the condition that Gratiano tame his characteristically wild behavior. Gratiano promises to be on his best behavior, and the two men plan a night of merriment to celebrate their departure.

SUMMARY: ACT II, SCENE III

Shylock's daughter Jessica bids good-bye to Launcelot. She tells him that his presence made life with her father more bearable. Jessica gives Launcelot a letter to carry to Bassanio's friend Lorenzo, and Launcelot leaves, almost too tearful to say good-bye. Jessica, left alone, confesses that although she feels guilty for being ashamed of her father, she is only his daughter by blood, and not by actions. Still, she hopes to escape her damning relationship to Shylock by marrying Lorenzo and converting to Christianity.

SUMMARY: ACT II, SCENE IV

On a street in Venice, Gratiano, Lorenzo, Salarino, and Solanio discuss the plan to unite Lorenzo with Jessica. Gratiano frets that they are not well prepared, but Lorenzo assures the men that they have enough time to gather the necessary disguises and torchbearers. As they talk, Launcelot enters bearing Jessica's letter. Lorenzo recognizes the writing, lovingly exclaiming that the hand that penned the message is "whiter than the paper it writ on" (II.iv.13). Lorenzo bids Launcelot to return to Shylock's house in order to assure Jessica, secretly, that Lorenzo will not let her down. Launcelot departs, and Lorenzo orders his friends to prepare for the night's festivities. Salarino and Solanio leave, and Lorenzo relates to Gratiano that Jessica will escape from Shylock's house by disguising herself as Lorenzo's torchbearer. Lorenzo gives Gratiano the letter and asks Gratiano to read it, then leaves, excited for the evening's outcome.

ANALYSIS: ACT II, SCENES I–IV

The elaborate excuse the prince of Morocco makes for his dark coloring serves to call attention to it and to his cultural difference from

Portia and from Shakespeare's audience. His extravagant praise of his own valor also makes him seem both less well-mannered and less attractive. Moreover, his assertion that the best virgins of his clime have loved him seems calculated to make him less, rather than more, attractive to Portia. Her response to his protestations is polite, even courtly, showing her good breeding and her virtuous acquiescence to her dead father's wishes. But her words also clearly convey that she does not want to marry him.

The scene between the Gobbos is typical of Shakespeare, who frequently employs servants and members of the working class to provide slapstick interludes in both his comedies and tragedies. *The Merchant of Venice* does not derive all of its comic moments from the malapropisms and double entendres of this odd father-son pair, but the humor here is more crass and vulgar—so simple that it is hard to overlook and mistake. Seen in this light, we forgive things that might otherwise seem cruel to us, like Launcelot's shabby treatment of his blind and doting father. This humor is comedy at its simplest, where laughs are derived not from quick wit but from confusion and foolery.

Although Shylock does not appear in these scenes, our view of him is further shaped by the opinions of those closest to him. Even though his servant and daughter do not like him, their descriptions of him inadvertently make him a more sympathetic figure in our eyes. Launcelot, we learn, is not abandoning his post because Shylock has proved to be a cruel or harsh master, but because he seems to fear contamination from being so close to a Jew. Interestingly, although he calls Shylock a devil, Launcelot points out that his desire to leave is a temptation more devilish still, and says his desire to stay is a product of his conscience, which is generally a guide of what is right. Jessica, too, voices no real complaint about her father, other than the tedium of life with him, but she seems eager to escape her Jewish heritage, which she sees as a stain on her honor. Jessica even brings the morality of her own actions into question when she calls her shame at being Shylock's daughter a sin, and she feels enormous guilt at her own sentiments. Her desire to convert would undoubtedly have been applauded by Elizabethan audiences, but here it is expressed as a kind of young recklessness that borders on selfishness. The negative impression that Shylock has given us with his first appearance is somewhat counteracted by the words of those closest to him, who feel guilty even as they speak ill of him.

ACT II, SCENES V–IX

SUMMARY: ACT II, SCENE V

Shylock warns Launcelot that Bassanio will not be as lenient a master as Shylock himself has been, and that Launcelot will no longer be at liberty to overeat and oversleep. Shylock calls for Jessica and tells her that he has been summoned for dinner. Worried by a premonition that trouble is brewing, Shylock asks Jessica to keep the doors locked and not look out at the revelry taking place in the streets. Launcelot whispers to Jessica that she must disobey her father and look out the window for the Christian who "will be worth a Jew's eye" (II.v.41). Shylock asks Jessica about her furtive conversation with Launcelot, and says that, though Launcelot is kind, he eats and sleeps too much to be an efficient, worthwhile servant. After Shylock has left to see Bassanio, Jessica bids him farewell, thinking that, if nothing goes wrong, Shylock will soon have lost a daughter, and she, a father.

SUMMARY: ACT II, SCENE VI

As planned, Gratiano and Salarino meet in front of Shylock's house. They are especially anxious because Lorenzo is late, and they think that lovers tend always to be early. The garrulous Gratiano expounds on Salarino's theory that love is at its best when the lover chases the object of his affection, and that once the lover captures his lady and consummates the relationship, he tends to tire and lose interest. Lorenzo joins them, apologizes for his tardiness, and calls up to Jessica, who appears on the balcony dressed as a page. Jessica tosses him a casket of gold and jewels. Jessica descends and exits with Lorenzo and Salarino. Just then, Antonio enters to report that Bassanio is sailing for Belmont immediately. Gratiano is obliged to leave the festivities and join Bassanio at once.

SUMMARY: ACT II, SCENE VII

Back in Belmont, Portia shows the prince of Morocco to the caskets, where he will attempt to win her hand by guessing which chest contains her portrait. The first casket, made of gold, is inscribed with the words, "Who chooseth me shall gain what many men desire" (II.vii.37). The second, made of silver, reads, "Who chooseth me shall get as much as he deserves" (II.vii.23). The third, a heavy leaden casket, declares, "Who chooseth me must give and hazard all he hath" (II.vii.16). After much pondering, the prince chooses the gold casket, reasoning that only the most precious metal could house the picture of such a beautiful woman. He opens the chest to reveal a skull with a scroll in its eye socket. After reading a short poem chastising him for the folly of his choice, the prince makes a hasty departure. Portia is glad to see him go and hopes that "[a]ll of his complexion choose me so" (II.viii.79).

SUMMARY: ACT II, SCENE VIII

Having witnessed Shylock's rage upon learning of Jessica's elopement, Solanio describes the scene to Salarino. Shylock, he reports, railed against the loss of his daughter and his ducats, and he shouted a loud, urgent appeal for justice and the law to prevail. Solanio hopes that Antonio is able to pay his debt, but Salarino reminds him of rumors that the long-awaited ships have capsized in the English Channel. The two men warmly remember Bassanio's departure from Antonio, wherein the merchant insisted that his young friend not allow thoughts of debt or danger to interfere with his courtship of Portia.

SUMMARY: ACT II, SCENE IX

The prince of Arragon is in Belmont to try his luck at winning Portia's hand in marriage. When brought to the caskets, he selects the silver one, confident that he "shall get as much as he deserves" (II. ix.35). Inside, he finds a portrait of a blinking idiot, and a poem that condemns him as a fool. Soon after he departs, a messenger arrives to tell Portia that a promising young Venetian, who seems like the perfect suitor, has come to Belmont to try his luck at the casket game. Hoping that it is Bassanio, Portia and Nerissa go out to greet the new suitor.

ANALYSIS: ACT II, SCENES V–IX

In these scenes, Shylock is again portrayed as a penny-pinching, but not wicked, master. Indeed, he seems to think himself quite lenient, and when he calls Launcelot lazy, this jibe seems likely to be an accurate description of the buffoonish retainer. Shylock's fear for his daughter and his distaste for the Venetian revelry paint him as a puritanical figure who respects order and the rule of law above all else, and who refuses to have "shallow fopp'ry" in his "sober house" (II. v.34–35). Shylock's rhetoric is distinctive: he tends to repeat himself and avoids the digressions common to other characters. As more than one critic has pointed out, he is characterized by a one-track mind.

Happily, Jessica and Lorenzo's romantic love triumphs, but a number of critics have pointed out the ambiguity in the scene of their elopement. The couple's love for one another is not in doubt, but Jessica's determination to bring a hefty store of treasure reminds us that she is still an alien, a Jew among gentiles, who may be insecure about her reception. Indeed, her shame at her boy's costume may reflect a deeper concern for her place in her husband's Christian society. Later, at Belmont, she will be all but ignored by everyone save Lorenzo, suggesting that despite her husband and her conversion, she remains a Jew in others' eyes.

The prince of Morocco's choice of the caskets is wrong, but his mistake is understandable, and we sympathize with him. There is something casually cruel about Portia's unwillingness to spare even a moment's pity for the Moor. Portia is a willful character—while her independence is often appealing, at other times she can seem terribly self-centered. She wants Bassanio as a husband and seems to have no regrets in seeing other suitors sentenced to a life of celibacy.

Salarino and Solanio are the least interesting characters in the play. They are indistinguishable from one another and serve primarily to fill us in on events that take place offstage—in this case, Shylock's reaction to his daughter's flight and the parting of Antonio and Bassanio. Shylock's cries of "My daughter! O, my ducats! O, my daughter!" are meant to be comic—the moneylender is, after all, a *comic* villain (II.viii.15). He bemoans the loss of his money as much as his loss of Jessica, suggesting that greed is as important to him as familial love. However, we cannot be sure that Shylock really reacted in this way, since we hear the story secondhand. Salarino and Solanio are poking fun at the Jew, and their testimony must be balanced by the concern that Shylock expresses for his daughter in the earlier scenes.

Arragon, a Spanish prince, completes the parade of nationalities competing for Portia. He lacks the nobility of the prince of Morocco, and his arrogance almost makes us feel that he deserves his punishment. His quick dismissal from the scene clears the way for Bassanio.

ACT III, SCENES I–II

SUMMARY: ACT III, SCENE I

> *Hath not a Jew hands, organs, dimensions, senses,*
> *affections, passions . . . ? If you prick us do we not*
> *bleed? If you tickle us do we not laugh? If you poison*
> *us do we not die? And if you wrong us shall we not*
> *revenge?*
>
> (See QUOTATIONS, p. 49)

Salarino and Solanio discuss the rumors that yet another of Antonio's ships has been wrecked. They are joined by Shylock, who accuses them of having helped Jessica escape. The two Venetians proudly take credit for their role in Jessica's elopement. Shylock curses his daughter's rebellion, to which Salarino responds, "There is more difference between thy flesh and hers than between jet and ivory" (III.i.32–33). Salarino then asks Shylock whether he can confirm the rumors of Antonio's lost vessels. Shylock replies that Antonio will soon be bankrupt and swears to collect his bond. Salarino doubts Shylock's resolve, wondering what the old man will do with a pound of flesh, to which Shylock chillingly replies that Antonio's flesh will at least feed his revenge. In a short monologue, Shylock says Antonio has mistreated him solely because Shylock is a Jew, but now Shylock is determined to apply the lessons of hatred and revenge that Christian intolerance has taught him so well.

Salarino and Solanio head off to meet with Antonio, just as Tubal, a friend of Shylock's and a Jew, enters. Tubal announces that he cannot find Jessica. Shylock rants against his daughter, and he wishes her dead as he bemoans his losses. He is especially embittered when Tubal reports that Jessica has taken a ring—given to Shylock in his bachelor days by a woman named Leah, presumably Jessica's mother—and has traded that ring for a monkey. Shylock's spirits brighten, however, when Tubal reports that Antonio's ships have run into trouble and that Antonio's creditors are certain Antonio is ruined.

SUMMARY: ACT III, SCENE II

In Belmont, Portia begs Bassanio to delay choosing between the caskets for a day or two. If Bassanio chooses incorrectly, Portia reasons, she will lose his company. Bassanio insists that he make his choice now, to avoid prolonging the torment of living without

Portia as his wife. Portia orders that music be played while her love makes his choice, and she compares Bassanio to the Greek hero and demigod Hercules. Like the suitors who have come before him, Bassanio carefully examines the three caskets and puzzles over their inscriptions. He rejects the gold casket, saying that "[t]he world is still deceived with ornament" (III.ii.74), while the silver he deems a "pale and common drudge / 'Tween man and man" (III.ii.103–104). After much debate, Bassanio picks the lead casket, which he opens to reveal Portia's portrait, along with a poem congratulating him on his choice and confirming that he has won Portia's hand.

The happy couple promises one another love and devotion, and Portia gives Bassanio a ring that he must never part with, as his removal of it will signify the end of his love for her. Nerissa and Gratiano congratulate them and confess that they too have fallen in love with one another. They suggest a double wedding. Lorenzo and Jessica arrive in the midst of this rejoicing, along with Salarino, who gives a letter to Bassanio. In the letter, Antonio writes that all of his ships are lost, and that Shylock plans to collect his pound of flesh. The news provokes a fit of guilt in Bassanio, which in turn prompts Portia to offer to pay twenty times the sum. Jessica, however, worries that her father is more interested in revenge than in money. Bassanio reads out loud the letter from Antonio, who asks only for a brief reunion before he dies. Portia urges her husband to rush to his friend's aid, and Bassanio leaves for Venice.

ANALYSIS: ACT III, SCENES I–II

The passage of time in *The Merchant of Venice* is peculiar. In Venice, the three months that Antonio has to pay the debt go by quickly, while only days seem to pass in Belmont. Shakespeare juggles these differing chronologies by using Salarino and Solanio to fill in the missing Venetian weeks.

As Antonio's losses mount, Shylock's villainous plan becomes apparent. "[L]et him look to his bond," he repeats single-mindedly (III.i.39–40). Despite his mounting obsession with the pound of Antonio's flesh, however, he maintains his dramatic dignity. In his scene with the pair of Venetians, he delivers the celebrated speech in which he cries, "Hath not a Jew eyes? Hath not a Jew hands, organs, dimensions, senses, affections, passions . . . ? If you prick us do we not bleed? If you tickle us do we not laugh? If you poison us do we not die?" (III.i.49–55). We are not meant to sympathize entirely with Shylock: he may have been wronged, but he lacks both mercy and a sense of proportion. His refusal to take pity on Antonio is later contrasted with the mercy shown him by the Christians. But even as we recognize that Shylock's plans are terribly wrong, we can appreciate the angry logic of his speech. By asserting his own humanity, he lays waste to the pretensions of the Christian characters to value mercy, charity, and love above self-interest.

Shylock's dignity lapses in his scene with Tubal, who keeps his supposed friend in agony by alternating between good and bad news. Shylock lurches from glee to despair and back, one moment crying, "I thank God, I thank God!" (III.i.86), and the next saying, "Thou stick'st a dagger in me" (III.i.92). But even here he rouses our sympathy, because we hear that Jessica stole a ring given to him by his late wife and traded it for a monkey. "It was my turquoise," Shylock says. "I had it of Leah when I was a bachelor. I would not have given it for a wilderness of monkeys" (III.i.100–103). Villain though he may be, we can still feel sorrow that Jessica—who is suddenly a much less sympathetic character—would be heartless enough to steal and sell a ring that her dead mother gave her father.

Bassanio's successful choice seems inevitable and brings the drama of the caskets to an end. Bassanio's excellence is made clear in his ability to select the correct casket, and his choice brings the separated strands of the plot together. Portia, who is the heroine of the play—she speaks far more lines than either Antonio or Shylock—is free to bring her will and intelligence to bear on the problem of Shylock's pound of flesh. Once Lorenzo and Jessica arrive, the three couples are together in Belmont, but the shadow of Shylock hangs over their happiness.

Critics have noticed that Jessica is ignored by Portia and the others at Belmont. Her testimony against her father may be an attempt to prove her loyalty to the Christian cause, but the coldness of Portia, Bassanio, and the others is an understandable reaction—after all, she is a Jew and the daughter of their antagonist. Lorenzo may love her, but she remains an object of suspicion for the others.

ACT III, SCENES III–V

SUMMARY: ACT III, SCENE III

Shylock escorts the bankrupt Antonio to prison. Antonio pleads with Shylock to listen, but Shylock refuses. Remembering the many times Antonio condemned him as a dog, Shylock advises the merchant to beware of his bite. Assured that the duke will grant him justice, Shylock insists that he will have his bond and tells the jailer not to bother speaking to him of mercy. Solanio declares that Shylock is the worst of men, and Antonio reasons that the Jew hates him for bailing out many of Shylock's debtors. Solanio attempts to comfort Antonio by suggesting that the duke will never allow such a ridiculous contract to stand, but Antonio is not convinced. Venice, Antonio claims, is a wealthy trading city with a great reputation for upholding the law, and if the duke breaks that law, Venice's economy may suffer. As Solanio departs, Antonio prays desperately that Bassanio will arrive to "see me pay his debt, and then I care not" (III.iii.36).

SUMMARY: ACT III, SCENE IV

Lorenzo assures Portia that Antonio is worthy of all the help she is sending him, and that if Portia only knew the depths of Antonio's love and goodness, she would be proud of her efforts to save him. Portia replies that she has never regretted doing a good deed, and goes on to say that she could never deny help to anyone so close to her dear Bassanio. Indeed, Antonio and Bassanio are so inseparable that Portia believes saving her husband's friend is no different than saving her own husband. She has sworn to live in prayer and contemplation until Bassanio returns to her, and announces that she and Nerissa will retire to a nearby monastery. Lorenzo and Jessica, she declares, will rule the estate in her absence.

Portia then sends her servant, Balthasar, to Padua, where he is to meet her cousin, Doctor Bellario, who will provide Balthasar with certain documents and clothing. From there, Balthasar will take the ferry to Venice, where Portia will await him. After Balthasar departs, Portia informs Nerissa that the two of them, dressed as young men, are going to pay an incognito visit to their new husbands. When Nerissa asks why, Portia dismisses the question, but promises to disclose the whole of her purpose on the coach ride to Venice.

SUMMARY: ACT III, SCENE V

Quoting the adage that the sins of the father shall be delivered upon the children, Launcelot says he fears for Jessica's soul. When Jessica claims that she will be saved by her marriage to Lorenzo, Launcelot complains that the conversion of the Jews, who do not eat pork, will have disastrous consequences on the price of bacon. Lorenzo enters and chastises Launcelot for impregnating a Moorish servant. Launcelot delivers a dazzling series of puns in reply and departs to prepare for dinner. When Lorenzo asks Jessica what she thinks of Portia, she responds that the woman is without match, nearly perfect in all respects. Lorenzo jokes that he is as good a spouse as Portia, and leads them off to dinner.

ANALYSIS: ACT III, SCENES III–V

Once the play reaches Act III, scene iii, it is difficult to sympathize with Shylock. Whatever humiliations he has suffered at Antonio's hands are repaid when he sees the Christian merchant in shackles. Antonio may have treated the moneylender badly, but Shylock's pursuit of the pound of flesh is an exercise in naked cruelty. In this scene, Shylock's narrowly focused rhetoric becomes monomaniacal in its obsession with the bond. "I'll have my bond. Speak not against my bond," (III.iii.4) he insists, and denies attempts at reason when he says, "I'll have no speaking. I will have my bond" (III.iii.17). When Antonio tells Solanio that Shylock is getting revenge for his practice of lending money without interest, he seems to miss the bigger picture. Shylock's mind has been warped into obsession not by Antonio alone, but by the persecutions visited on him by all of Christian Venice. He has taken Antonio as the embodiment of all his persecutors so that, in his pound of flesh, he can avenge himself against *everyone*.

The institution of law comes to the forefront of the play in these scenes, and we may be tempted to view the law as a sort of necessary evil, a dogmatic set of rules that can be forced to serve the most absurd requests. In the thirty-six lines that make up Act III, scene iii, Shylock alludes to revenge in only the vaguest of terms, but repeats the word "bond" no less than six times. He also frequently invokes the concept of justice. Law is cast as the very backbone of the Venetian economy, as Antonio expresses when he makes the grim statement that "[t]he duke cannot deny the course of law. . . . / . . . / Since that the trade and profit of the city / Consisteth of all nations" (III.iii.26–31). Trade is the city's lifeblood, and an integral part of trade is ensuring that merchants of all religions and nationalities are extended the same protections as full-blooded Venetian citizens. In principle, the duke's inability to bend the law is sound, as the law upholds the economy that has allowed Antonio and his friends to thrive. However, Shylock's furious rants about justice and his bond make it seem as if his very law-abiding nature has perverted a bastion of Christian uprightness.

Shylock remains in control of events in Venice, but Portia, his antagonist, is now moving against him. Her cross-dressing is a device typical of women in Shakespeare's comedies. Indeed, the play has already shown Jessica dressed as a boy in her escape from Shylock's house. Dressing as a man is necessary since Portia is about to play a man's part, appearing as member of a male profession. The demands placed upon her by her father's will are gone, and she feels free to act and to prove herself more intelligent and capable than the men around her.

The conversation between Jessica and Launcelot in Act III, scene v, does little to advance the plot. It acts as comic relief and conveys the impression of time passing while the various characters converge on the Venetian courtroom. Jessica's subsequent description of Portia's perfection to her husband is odd, given how little attention Portia paid to her, but Jessica recognizes that Portia is the center of the social world that she hopes to join.

ACT IV, SCENE I, LINES 1–163

SUMMARY

> ... [A]ffection,
> Mistress of passion, sways it to the mood
> Of what it likes or loathes.
> ...
> So can I give no reason, nor I will not,
> More than a lodged hate and a certain loathing
> I bear Antonio, that I follow thus
> A losing suit against him. Are you answered?
>
> (See QUOTATIONS, p. 50)

In Venice, the Court convenes for Antonio's trial. The duke of Venice greets Antonio and expresses pity for him, calling Shylock an inhuman monster who can summon neither pity nor mercy. Antonio says he knows the duke has done all that he can to lawfully counter Shylock's malicious intentions, and that since nothing else can be done, Antonio will respond to Shylock's rage "with a quietness of spirit" (IV.i.11). The duke summons Shylock into the courtroom and addresses him, saying that he believes that Shylock means only to frighten Antonio by extending this drama to the brink of performance. No one, the duke says, believes that Shylock actually means to inflict such a horrible penalty on Antonio, who has already suffered the loss of his ships. Shylock reiterates his intentions and says that should the court deny him his right, the city's very laws and freedoms will be forfeit. Shylock offers no explanation for his insistence other than to say that certain hatreds, like certain passions, are lodged deep within a person's heart. Shylock hates Antonio, and for him that is reason enough.

Bassanio, who has arrived from Belmont, attempts to argue with Shylock, but Antonio tells him that his efforts are for naught. Hatred and predation, Antonio suggests, come as naturally to some men as they do to the wolf. Bassanio offers Shylock six thousand ducats, twice the amount of the original loan, but Shylock turns down the offer, saying he would not forfeit his bond for six times that sum. When the duke asks Shylock how he expects to receive mercy when he offers none, Shylock replies that he has no need for mercy, as he has done nothing wrong. Just as the slave-owning Christians of Venice would refuse to set their human property free, Shylock will not relinquish the pound of flesh that belongs to him.

The duke says that he has sent messages to the learned lawyer, Doctor Bellario, asking him to come and decide on the matter. News comes that a messenger has arrived from Bellario, and Salarino runs off to fetch him. Meanwhile, Bassanio tries, without much success, to cheer up the despairing Antonio. Nerissa enters, disguised as a lawyer's clerk, and gives the duke a letter from Bellario. Shylock whets his knife, anticipating a judgment in his favor, and Gratiano accuses him of having the soul of a wolf. Shylock ignores these slurs and states resolutely, "I stand here for law" (IV.i.141). The duke alludes to the fact that Bellario's letter mentions a learned young lawyer named Balthasar, and orders the disguised Nerissa to admit the young man to the court. The duke then reads the letter in its entirety. In it, Bellario writes that he is ill and cannot come to court, but that he has sent the learned young Balthasar to judge in his stead.

> You will answer 'The slaves are ours.' So do I answer you.
> The pound of flesh which I demand of him
> Is dearly bought. 'Tis mine, and I will have it.
> *(See* QUOTATIONS, *p. 51)*

ANALYSIS

The trial scene is the longest in the play and stands as one of the most dramatic scenes in all of Shakespeare. A number of critics have raised questions about the accuracy and fairness of the courtroom proceedings: the presiding duke is far from impartial; Portia appears as an unbiased legal authority, when in fact she is married to the defendant's best friend; and she appears in disguise, under a false name. These points would seem to stack the deck against Shylock, but if the trial is not just, then the play is not just, and it ceases to be a comedy. Thus, while Portia bends the rules of the court, her decision is nonetheless legally accurate. More important for the cause of justice, the original bond was made under false pretenses—Shylock lied when he told Antonio that he would never collect the pound of flesh. Therefore, Portia's actions restore justice instead of pervert it.

The portion of the scene that passes before Portia's entrance shows a triumphant and merciless Shylock. When asked to explain his reasons for wanting Antonio's flesh, he says, "I am not bound to please thee with my answers" (IV.i.64). The only answer that the court gets, ultimately, is that Shylock merely emulates Christian behavior. Just as some Christians hate cats, pigs, and rats, Shylock hates Antonio. Just as some Christians own slaves, Shylock owns a pound of Antonio's flesh. Shylock has the law on his side, and his chief emotion seems to be outrage that Christian Venice would deny him what is rightfully his. Shylock is not so much attacking the Venetian worldview as demanding that he be allowed to share in it. His speech about slavery is emphatically *not* an antislavery diatribe: he is in favor owning people, as long as he can own Antonio. In spite of itself, Venetian society is made an accomplice to Shylock's murderous demands, and while this complicity certainly does not exonerate Shylock, it has the almost equally desirable effect of bringing everyone else down with him. Shylock's intention is not to condemn the institution of slavery, and certainly not to urge its eradication—it is to express that his urges simply mirror those already found among wealthy Venetians, and to demand that his desires be greeted with the same respect.

The trial is not modeled on the English legal system. The duke presides and sentences, but a legal expert—in this case, Portia—renders the actual decision. This absolute power is appropriate for her character because she alone has the strength to wield it. None of the men seem a match for Shylock: Gratiano shouts and curses with anti-Semitic energy, Bassanio pleads uselessly, and Antonio seems resigned to his fate. Indeed, Antonio seems almost eager for his execution, saying, "I am a tainted wether of the flock, / Meetest for death" (IV.i.113–114). Antonio has been melancholy from the play's beginning, and now he has found a cause to suit his unhappiness. He may be the focus of Shylock's hate, but he is less an antagonist than a victim. It is left to Portia to put a stop to the moneylender and to restore the comedy—something in short supply in Shylock's courtroom—to the play.

ACT IV, SCENE I, LINES 164–396

SUMMARY

> *. . . Therefore, Jew,*
> *Though justice be thy plea, consider this:*
> *That in the course of justice none of us*
> *Should see salvation. We do pray for mercy,*
> *And that same prayer doth teach us all to render*
> *The deeds of mercy. . . .*
>
> (See QUOTATIONS, p. 52)

Portia enters, disguised as Balthasar. The duke greets her and asks whether she is familiar with the circumstances of the case. Portia answers that she knows the case well, and the duke calls Shylock and Antonio before her. Portia asks Antonio if he admits to owing Shylock money. When Antonio answers yes, Portia concludes that the Jew must be merciful. Shylock asks why he must show mercy, and, in one of the play's most famous speeches, Portia responds that "[t]he quality of mercy is not strained," but is a blessing to both those who provide and those who receive it (IV.i.179). Because mercy is an attribute of God, Portia reasons, humans approach the divine when they exercise it. Shylock brushes aside her pretty speech, however, by reiterating his demands for justice and revenge.

Portia asks whether Antonio is able to pay the money, and Bassanio offers Shylock twice the sum owed. If need be, Bassanio says, he is willing to pay the bond ten times over, or with his own life. Bassanio begs the court to bend the law slightly in order to exonerate Antonio, reasoning that such a small infraction is a little wrong for a great right. Portia replies, however, that the law shall not be broken—the decrees of Venice must stand. Shylock joyfully extols Portia's wisdom, and gives her the bond for inspection. She looks it over, declares it legal and binding, and bids Shylock to be merciful. Shylock remains deaf to reason, however, and Portia tells Antonio to prepare himself for the knife. She orders Shylock to have a surgeon on hand to prevent the merchant from bleeding to death, but Shylock refuses because the bond stipulates no such safeguard.

Antonio bids Bassanio farewell. He asks his friend not to grieve for him and tells Bassanio that he is happy to sacrifice his life, if only to prove his love. Both Bassanio and Gratiano say that, though they love their wives, they would give them up in order to save Antonio. In a pair of sarcastic asides, Portia and Nerissa mutter that Bassanio's and Gratiano's wives are unlikely to appreciate such sentiments. Shylock is on the verge of cutting into Antonio when Portia suddenly reminds him that the bond stipulates a pound of flesh only, and makes no allowances for blood. She urges Shylock to continue collecting his pound of flesh, but reminds him that if a drop of blood is spilled, then he will be guilty of conspiring against the life of a Venetian citizen and all his lands and goods will be confiscated by the state. Stunned, Shylock hastily backpedals, agreeing to accept three times the sum, but Portia is insistent, saying that Shylock must have the pound of flesh or nothing. When Shylock finds out that he cannot even take the original three thousand ducats in place of the pound of flesh, he drops the case, but Portia stops him, reminding him of the penalty that noncitizens face when they threaten the life of a Venetian. In such a case, Portia states, half of Shylock's property would go to the state, while the other half would go to the offended party—namely, Antonio. Portia orders Shylock to beg for the duke's mercy.

The duke declares that he will show mercy: he spares Shylock's life and demands only a fine, rather than half of the Jew's estate. Shylock claims that they may as well take his life, as it is worthless without his estate. Antonio offers to return his share of Shylock's estate, on the condition that Shylock convert to Christianity and bequeath all his goods to Jessica and Lorenzo upon his death. Shylock consents and departs, saying simply, "I am not well" (IV.i.392).

ANALYSIS

In the course of this section of Act IV, scene i, Portia not only releases Antonio from his bond, but effectively strips Shylock of both his religion and his livelihood, rendering him unable to inflict, or even threaten, further damage. This outcome is a little surprising given that the circumstances of the trial seem designed to ensure Shylock's defeat. The genre of comedy demands that Shakespeare dispatch his villain before ushering in a happy ending. Indeed, Shakespeare's sixteenth-century audience never doubts Shylock's fate. Neither the duke, who begins proceedings by declaring Shylock an "inhuman wretch," nor the disguised Portia are impartial judges (IV.i.3). Shylock must fall, and fall he certainly does, but our response to witnessing his fall may be mixed. Audiences in Elizabethan England most likely met Shylock's demise with something like

Gratiano's cruel and ecstatic glee. In a society that not only craved cultural homogeneity but took drastic measures to attain it, few would have been troubled by the implications of Shylock's forced conversion. Shakespeare's contemporaries, the majority of whom assumed that eternal damnation was the fate of any non-Christian, would have witnessed Shylock's conversion as a vital contribution to the play's happy ending. By turning Shylock into a Christian, the Venetians satisfy themselves with their own kindness in saving the soul of a heathen. Audiences today find laughing at Shylock to be much harder.

Many readers find it difficult to rejoice in Portia's victory. Ultimately, Shylock's pursuit of a strict letter-of-the-law brand of justice, which makes no allowance for anything that even approaches compassion, undoes him. He proves blind to everything other than the stipulations of his bond, refusing even to summon a doctor to attend to Antonio's wounds. But we may feel that the punishment Portia exacts is too heavy. Perhaps the court's verdict fits Shylock's crimes, but the court indulges in an equally literal and severe reading of the law in order to effect the same vicious end: the utter annihilation of a human being. Before doling out Shylock's punishment, the duke assures him that he will "see the difference of our spirit," but the spirit of the Venetians proves to be as vindictive as the Jew's (IV.i.363). The duke spares Shylock's life, but takes away his ability to practice his profession and his religion. In the course of the play, Shylock has lost his servant, his daughter, his fortune, and a treasured ring given to him by his dead wife. He will forfeit his estate to the man responsible for stealing his daughter, and he will abandon his religion for one that forbids him from practicing the trade by which he earns his livelihood. Modern audiences cannot help but view Shylock as a victim. He has become a tragic figure in a comedy that has no place for a character so complex.

ACT IV, SCENE I, LINES 397–453; SCENE II

SUMMARY: ACT IV, SCENE I, LINES 397–453

After Shylock leaves, the duke invites Portia, still in the disguise of a young lawyer, to dinner. Portia declines, saying that she must leave immediately for Padua. As she leaves, the duke tells Antonio to reward the young law clerk, since it was he who saved Antonio's life. Bassanio thanks Portia, though he does not see through her disguise, and offers her the money he brought with him in order to pay off Shylock. Portia declines the gift and says that having delivered Antonio from Shylock's clutches is payment enough. Bassanio insists that she take some token from him, and she eventually agrees. Portia asks Antonio for his gloves and Bassanio for his ring, which she herself gave Bassanio on the condition that he never part with it. Bassanio pulls his hand away, calling the ring a trifle and claiming that he will not dishonor the judge by giving him such a lowly gift. Instead, Bassanio offers to find the most valuable ring in Venice, but Portia remains firm, and demands the trifle or nothing. When Bassanio admits that the ring was a gift from his wife, who made him promise never to part with it, Portia claims that the excuse is convenient and used by many men to hold onto possessions they would rather not lose. With that, she takes her leave. Antonio urges Bassanio to let the law clerk have the ring, saying that he should value Antonio's love and the gentleman's worth more than his wife's orders. Bassanio gives in and sends Gratiano to run after Portia and present her with the ring. Antonio and Bassanio then leave for Antonio's house to plan their trip to Belmont.

SUMMARY: ACT IV, SCENE II

Meanwhile, Portia sends Nerissa to Shylock's house to ensure that Shylock signs the deed that will leave his fortune to Lorenzo and Jessica. Portia observes that Lorenzo will be happy to have this document. Once they complete this task, the disguised women plan to leave for Belmont, which will ensure their arrival a full day before their husbands'. Gratiano enters, offers Bassanio's ring to Portia, and invites her to dinner. Portia accepts the ring, but declines the invitation. Portia asks Gratiano to show Nerissa to Shylock's house, and Nerissa, before leaving, tells Portia that she will likewise try to convince Gratiano to part with his ring. The plan satisfies Portia, who imagines how Gratiano and Bassanio will swear up and down that they gave their rings to men, and looks forward to embarrassing them. Nerissa turns to Gratiano and asks him to lead her to Shylock's house.

ANALYSIS: ACT IV, SCENE I, LINES 397–453; SCENE II

By the end of Act IV, Shakespeare has resolved the play's two primary plots: the casket game has delivered to Portia her rightful suitor, and the threat presented by Shylock has been eliminated. Structurally, this resolution makes *The Merchant of Venice* atypical of Shakespeare's comedies, which usually feature a wedding as a means of dispelling evils from and restoring rightness to the world. Here, however, the lovers are already wed, and the aftertaste of Shylock's trial is rather bitter, especially to modern audiences. In order to sweeten his story, returning us to the unmistakable province of comedy, Shakespeare launches a third plot involving the exchange of the rings. Perhaps Shakespeare recognized the ambivalence with which we would greet Shylock's demise and felt the need to reassert simple joy over the dark dramas of Venice. Life in blissful Belmont depends upon it.

Many critics have noted that the character of Shylock necessitates this rather forced return to the comedic. As one of Shakespeare's most powerful and memorable creations, Shylock looms large over the play, and though he is not seen again after exiting the court, he remains lodged in our memory. In order for the lovers to enjoy a typically unadulterated happy ending, the angry, potentially victimized specter of Shylock must first be exorcised from the stage. The ring game is Shakespeare's means of reasserting levity. Many critics consider Shylock a character who "ran away" from the playwright. Shylock may have started out as a familiar character: a two-dimensional villain in the red fright wig that European Jews were once required to wear. However, he emerges as an extremely intelligent man who has suffered profound mistreatment. Shakespeare provides Shylock with motivation for his malice, which raises Shylock above the level of evildoing bogeyman and makes his passions, no matter how terrible, at least comprehensible. For this reason, few modern audiences cheer when the Venetian court destroys Shylock. Our response to the Jew's demise is likely to be much more complicated and ambivalent. The lovers' exchange of the rings helps reposition the play as a comedy.

In devising the game in which Bassanio sacrifices his wedding ring, Portia once again proves herself cleverer and more competent than any of the men with whom she shares the stage. The ring game tests the boundaries of the homoerotic relationship between Antonio and Bassanio, for Antonio claims that his friend's love for him should "[b]e valued 'gainst your wife's commandment" (IV.i.447). Bassanio's willingness to part with the ring might signal a form of infidelity to his wife, but we feel little anxiety over it. Once Shylock makes his way offstage, the mood of the play is decidedly light. In other words, boundaries are tested, but they are not crossed. As the comedy genre demands, whatever wrongs have been committed will be forgiven summarily. When, at the end of Act IV, scene ii, Portia tells Nerissa that "we shall have old swearing / That they did give the rings away to men. / But we'll outface them, and outswear them too," we anticipate a frolicsome display of Portia's wit, not an untimely and costly battle of irreconcilable differences (IV.ii.15–17).

Act V, scene i

Summary

> The man that hath no music in himself,
> Nor is not moved with concord of sweet sounds,
> Is fit for treasons, stategems, and spoils.
> The motions of his spirit are dull as night,
> And his affections dark as Erebus.
>
> (See QUOTATIONS, p. 53)

In moonlit Belmont, Jessica and Lorenzo compare themselves to famous lovers from classical literature, like Troilus and Cressida, Pyramus and Thisbe, and Dido and Aeneas. The couple goes back and forth with endless declarations of love, when a messenger suddenly interrupts them. The messenger informs them that Portia will soon return from the monastery, and Lorenzo and Jessica prepare to greet the mistress of the house. Launcelot enters and announces that Bassanio will return to Belmont the next day. Lorenzo calls for music, and he and Jessica sit on a grassy bank beneath the stars. Lorenzo contemplates the music made by the movement of heavenly orbs, which mortal humans cannot hear while alive. The musicians arrive and begin to play, and Lorenzo decides that anyone who is not moved by music deserves the worst cruelties and betrayals.

Portia and Nerissa enter and hear the music before they reach the estate. Portia believes that the music is made more beautiful by the night, and the flickering candles lighting up her estate enchant her. She decides that the worth of things is determined largely by the context in which they are experienced. Lorenzo greets Portia, and she requests that he not mention her absence to her husband. Trumpets sound as Bassanio, Antonio, and Gratiano arrive. Portia greets Bassanio, who introduces her to Antonio, who reports in turn that he has been acquitted in the courts of Venice. Gratiano and Nerissa begin to argue over the ring with which he promised never to part. Nerissa chastises her husband not for hurting her feelings, but for breaking his own promise. Gratiano insists that he gave the ring to a lawyer's clerk as a fee, and Portia criticizes him for parting with so precious a gift, saying that her own husband would never have parted with his ring. Gratiano corrects her and reveals that Bassanio has, in fact, given his ring to the lawyer who saved Antonio. Portia declares that her husband's heart is as empty as his finger, and she promises never to visit his bed until he produces the ring.

Bassanio pleads with Portia to understand that he gave the ring to a worthy man to whom he was indebted, but Portia dismisses his reasoning, saying it is more likely that Bassanio gave the ring to another woman. Portia vows to be equally unfaithful, threatening to offer the same worthy man anything she owns, including her body or her husband's bed. Antonio intercedes on behalf of Bassanio and Gratiano, asking the women to accept his soul should either Bassanio or Gratiano prove unfaithful again. Portia and Nerissa relent, giving each of their husbands a ring and suggesting that they exercise more care in keeping these rings. Bassanio and Gratiano recognize these as the same rings they gave to the lawyer and his clerk, and Portia and Nerissa claim that they lay with the gentlemen in order to get back the rings. Before either Bassanio or Gratiano can become too upset at being cuckolded, however, Portia reveals that she was the lawyer in Venice, and Nerissa her clerk. Antonio receives news that some of his ships have miraculously arrived in port, and Lorenzo is told that he will inherit Shylock's fortune. The company rejoices in its collective good fortune.

SUMMARY & ANALYSIS

ANALYSIS

In comparison to the preceding trial scene, Act V is decidedly lighter in tone. The play delivers the happy ending required of a comedy: the lovers are restored to their loving relationships, Antonio's supposedly lost ships arrive miraculously in port, and no threatening presence looms in the distance to suggest that this happiness is only temporary. The idyllic quality of life in Belmont has led some critics to declare that *The Merchant of Venice* is a "fairy story" into which the dark and dramatic figure of Shylock trespasses. Certainly the language of the play returns to the realm of comedic romance after Shylock's departure. Before Shylock shocks the play with his morbid reality, Salarino is free to envision a shipwreck as a lovely scattering of "spices on the stream" (I.i.33). Now that Shylock has been banished, Lorenzo imagines that the each star in the sky produces music as it moves, "choiring to the young-eyed cherubins" (V.i.61). In describing the "sweet power of music" to Jessica, Lorenzo claims that such sounds have the ability to tame even the wildest beasts (V.i.78). Thus, as the music plays on the hills of Belmont, the characters seem confident that the forces requiring taming—Shylock and his blood-lust—have been suppressed, leaving them to enjoy the "concord of sweet sounds" (V.i.83).

But if the play's end seems reminiscent of a fairy tale, it is also likely to evoke some of the same ambivalence with which we greet Shylock's demise. For example, Jessica and Lorenzo begin Act V by comparing themselves to a catalogue of famous lovers. They mean to place themselves in a pantheon of romantic figures whose love was so great that it inspired praise from generations of poets, but all of the lovers named—Troilus and Cressida, Pyramus and Thisbe, Dido and Aeneas, Medea and Jason—end tragically. Newlyweds should not necessarily hope to take their place in this lineup, as it promises misunderstanding, betrayal, and death.

Shakespeare spares us such tragedy, but he does load the ending with misunderstanding and betrayal, albeit in a comic form. Portia and Nerissa work their husbands into a frenzy, but they also know when to stop. As soon as Bassanio declares himself a cuckold, Portia begs him to "[s]peak not so grossly" and unveils the means by which she secured his ring (V.i.265). Thus, Bassanio and Gratiano are folded back into their wives' good graces. The play ends with Gratiano asserting that "while I live I'll fear no other thing / So sore as keeping safe Nerissa's ring" (V.i.305–306). The line suggests that he will not only safeguard the band of gold his wife gave him, but will also strive to keep her sexually satisfied so that she has no reason to cuckold him. But here, too, a shadow steals over the finale of celebratory reconciliation, for we wonder if Bassanio and Gratiano have what it takes to keep up with their wives. Nowhere in the play—not even when Bassanio chooses the correct casket—do the men come close to matching Portia's wit or cleverness. Although Shakespeare leaves these issues offstage, we cannot help but feel that dangers have not so much been expelled from the world as kept at bay. Happiness reigns in Belmont, if only for the time being. As Portia approaches her estate to find a candle burning brightly, she notes with surprise, "How far that little candle throws his beams— / So shines a good deed in a naughty world" (V.i.89–90). Here, she frames a glimmer of light, of happiness or hope, as a surprisingly beautiful but always temporary condition in a dark and dangerous world. As far as happy endings go, perhaps we can ask for little more.

IMPORTANT QUOTATIONS
EXPLAINED

1. I am a Jew. Hath not a Jew eyes? Hath not a Jew hands,
    organs, dimensions, senses, affections, passions; fed with
    the same food, hurt with the same weapons, subject to the
    same diseases, healed by the same means, warmed and
    cooled by the same winter and summer as a Christian is?
    If you prick us do we not bleed? If you tickle us do we not
    laugh? If you poison us do we not die? And if you wrong
    us shall we not revenge? If we are like you in the rest, we
    will resemble you in that. If a Jew wrong a Christian, what
    is his humility? Revenge. If a Christian wrong a Jew, what
    should his sufferance be by Christian example? Why,
    revenge. The villainy you teach me I will execute, and it
    shall go hard but I will better the instruction.

    (III.i.49–61)

There are perhaps fewer disturbing lines in all of Shakespeare than
Shylock's promise to Solanio and Salarino in Act III, scene i, that
he will outdo the evil that has been done to him. Shylock begins by
eloquently reminding the Venetians that all people, even those who
are not part of the majority culture, are human. A Jew, he reasons,
is equipped with the same faculties as a Christian, and is therefore
subject to feeling the same pains and comforts and emotions. The
speech, however, is not a celebration of shared experience or even an
invitation for the Venetians to acknowledge their enemy's humanity.
Instead of using reason to elevate himself above his Venetian torment-
ers, Shylock delivers a monologue that allows him to sink to their
level: he will, he vows, behave as villainously as they have. The speech
is remarkable in that it summons a range of emotional responses to
Shylock. At first, we doubtlessly sympathize with the Jew, whose right
to fair and decent treatment has been so neglected by the Venetians
that he must remind them that he has "hands, organs, dimensions,
senses" similar to theirs (III.i.50). But Shylock's pledge to behave as
badly as they, and, moreover, to "better the instruction," casts him in
a less sympathetic light (III.i.61). While we understand his motivation, we cannot excuse the endless perpetuation of such villainy.

49

2.   What if my house be troubled with a rat,
      And I be pleased to give ten thousand ducats
      To have it baned? What, are you answered yet?
      Some men there are love not a gaping pig,
      Some that are mad if they behold a cat,
      And others when the bagpipe sings i'th' nose
      Cannot contain their urine; for affection,
      Mistress of passion, sways it to the mood
      Of what it likes or loathes. . . .
      . . .
      So can I give no reason, nor I will not,
      More than a lodged hate and a certain loathing
      I bear Antonio, that I follow thus
      A losing suit against him. Are you answered?

                                              (IV.i.43–61)

When, in Act IV, scene i, Antonio and Shylock are summoned before
the court, the duke asks the Jew to show his adversary some mercy.
Shylock responds by reasoning that he has no reason. He blames
his hatred of Antonio on "affection, / [that] Mistress of passion,"
who is known to affect men's moods in ways they cannot explain
(IV.i.49–50). Just as certain people do not know why they have an
aversion to cats or certain strains of music or eating meat, Shylock
cannot logically explain his dislike for Antonio. The whole of his
response to the court boils down to the terribly eloquent equivalent
of the simple answer: just because. The speech merits consideration
not only because it articulates a range of emotions that often cannot
be verbally expressed, but also because Shylock's language patterns
reinforce our impression of his character. The use of repetition in the
passage is frequent. Shylock returns not only to the same imagery—
the "gaping pig" (IV.i.53) and the "woolen bagpipe" (IV.i.55)—but
he also bookends his speech with the simple question, "Are you an-
swered?" (IV.i.61). Here, Shylock's tightly controlled speech reflects
the narrow and determined focus of his quest to satisfy his hatred.

    The speech's imagery is of the prosaic sort typical of Shylock.
Other characters speak in dreamily poetic tones, evoking images
of angels and waters scented with spice, but Shylock draws on the
most mundane examples to prove his point. To him, Antonio is a
rat, and his dislike of Antonio no more odd than that which some
men have toward pigs or cats. Shylock uses bodily functions to drive
home his point, likening rage to urination in a crass turn of phrase

that is unique to his character. Also, Shylock's rage takes on an apparent arbitrariness. Originally, Shylock's gripe with Antonio seems based on a carefully meditated catalogue of the Venetian's crimes. Here, however, it appears little more than a whim, a swing of the pendulum that "sways" to affection's moods (IV.i.50). By relying on the defense that his actions are justified simply because he feels like them, Shylock appears unpredictable and whimsical, and he further fuels our perception of his actions as careless and cruel.

3.   You have among you many a purchased slave
        Which, like your asses and your dogs and mules,
        You use in abject and in slavish parts
        Because you bought them. Shall I say to you
        'Let them be free, marry them to your heirs.
        Why sweat they under burdens?. . .
        . . .
           You will answer
        'The slaves are ours.' So do I answer you.
        The pound of flesh which I demand of him
        Is dearly bought. 'Tis mine, and I will have it.

                                 (IV.i.89–99)

Again, in this passage, we find Shylock cleverly using Venice's own laws to support his vengeful quest and enlisting society's cruelties in defense of his own. Shylock begins his speech on a humane note, yet this opening serves merely to justify his indulgence in the same injustices he references. Shylock has no interest in exposing the wrongfulness of owning or mistreating slaves. Such property rights simply happen to be established by Venetian laws, so Shylock uses them to appeal for equal protection. If Antonio and company can purchase human flesh to "use in abject and in slavish parts," Shylock reasons, then he can purchase part of the flesh of a Venetian citizen (IV.i.91). In his mind, he has merely extended the law to its most literal interpretation. Unlike the Venetians, who are willing to bend or break the law to satisfy their wants, Shylock never strays from its letter in his pursuit of his bond. His brand of abiding by the law, however, is made unsavory by the gruesome nature of his interpretation.

4.   The quality of mercy is not strained.
       It droppeth as the gentle rain from heaven
       Upon the place beneath. . . .
       . . .
       It is enthronèd in the hearts of kings;
       It is an attribute to God himself,
       And earthly power doth then show likest God's
       When mercy seasons justice. Therefore, Jew,
       Though justice be thy plea, consider this:
       That in the course of justice none of us
       Should see salvation. We do pray for mercy,
       And that same prayer doth teach us all to render
       The deeds of mercy.

                                              (IV.i.179–197)

Even as she follows the standard procedure of asking Shylock
for mercy, Portia reveals her skills by appealing to his methodical
mind. Her argument draws on a careful process of reasoning rather
than emotion. She states first that the gift of forgiving the bond
would benefit Shylock, and second, that it would elevate Shylock
to a godlike status. Lastly, Portia warns Shylock that his quest for
justice without mercy may result in his own damnation. Although
well-measured and well-reasoned, Portia's speech nonetheless casts
mercy as a polarizing issue between Judaism and Christianity. Her
frequent references to the divine are appeals to a clearly Christian
God, and mercy emerges as a marker of Christianity. Although it
seems as if Portia is offering an appeal, in retrospect her speech
becomes an ultimatum, a final chance for Shylock to save himself
before Portia crushes his legal arguments.

5. The man that hath no music in himself,
    Nor is not moved with concord of sweet sounds,
    Is fit for treasons, stategems, and spoils.
    The motions of his spirit are dull as night,
    And his affections dark as Erebus.

                                        (V.i.82–86)

By Act V, with Shylock stowed safely offstage, Shakespeare returns to the comedic aspects of his play. He lightens the mood with a harmless exchange of rings that serves to reunite the lovers, and he brings Antonio's lost ships back to port. Because Shylock has been such a large, powerful presence in the play, and because his decimation at the hands of the Venetians is profoundly disturbing, the comedy in Belmont never fully escapes the shadow of the troublesome issues that precede it. The lovers' happiness, then, is most likely little more than a brief passing moment. This passage can be read as a meditation on the transitory nature of the comforts one finds in a wearisome world. Lorenzo, ordering music to celebrate Portia's homecoming, reflects that music has the power to change a man's nature. Much like a wild beast that can be tamed by the sound of a trumpet, a man can be transformed into something less "stockish, hard, and full of rage" (V.i.80). As the Venetians, all of whom have exercised "treasons, strategems, and spoils" of one kind or another throughout the play, congregate at Belmont, we imagine them as kinder and happier than they have otherwise been, but we also know that the music of Belmont will not likely survive on the streets of Venice (V.i.84).

KEY FACTS

FULL TITLE
The Comical History of the Merchant of Venice, or Otherwise Called the Jew of Venice

AUTHOR
William Shakespeare

TYPE OF WORK
Play

GENRE
Comedy

LANGUAGE
English

TIME AND PLACE WRITTEN
1598; London, England

DATE OF FIRST PUBLICATION
First published in the Quarto of 1600

PUBLISHER
I. R. for Thomas Heys

TONE
Comic, romantic, tragic

SETTING (TIME)
Sixteenth century

SETTING (PLACE)
Venice and Belmont, Italy

PROTAGONIST
There is no clear protagonist. Antonio is the merchant of the play's title, but he plays a relatively passive role. The major struggles of the play are Bassanio's quest to marry Portia and his attempt to free Antonio from Shylock, so Bassanio is the likeliest candidate.

MAJOR CONFLICT

Antonio defaults on a loan he borrowed from Shylock, wherein he promises to sacrifice a pound of flesh.

RISING ACTION

Antonio's ships, the only means by which he can pay off his debt to Shylock, are reported lost at sea.

CLIMAX

Portia, disguised as a man of law, intervenes on Antonio's behalf.

FALLING ACTION

Shylock is ordered to convert to Christianity and bequeath his possessions to Lorenzo and Jessica; Portia and Nerissa persuade their husbands to give up their rings

THEMES

Self-interest versus love; the divine quality of mercy; hatred as a cyclical phenomenon

MOTIFS

The law; cross-dressing; filial piety

SYMBOLS

The pound of flesh; Leah's ring; the three caskets

FORESHADOWING

In the play's opening scene, Shakespeare foreshadows Antonio's grim future by suggesting both his indebtedness to a creditor and the loss of his valuable ships.

STUDY QUESTIONS

1. *Discuss Shylock's dramatic function in* THE
   MERCHANT OF VENICE. *What do critics mean when
   they suggest that Shylock is "too large" for the play?
   Does he fulfill or exceed his role?*

In order to ensure that we understand Shylock as a threat to the happiness of Venice's citizens and lovers, Shakespeare uses a number of dramatic devices to amplify Shylock's villainy. In doing so, however, he creates a character so compelling that many feel Shylock comes to dominate the play, thereby making him "too large." Certainly, Shylock is a masterful creation. At his cruelest, he is terrifying, even more so because all of his schemes exist within the framework of the law. Seen in this light, Shylock becomes a kind of bogeyman, turning Venetian society's own institutions on themselves. On the other hand, Shylock is also pitiable, even sympathetic, at times. He has been harshly handled by Venetian society and has seen his daughter elope with one of the same men who despise him. His passionate monologue in Act III, scene i reveals that he feels the same emotions as his opponents, and we cannot help but see him as a man. In fact, Shylock's character is so well-rounded and intricate that many see him as the only interesting figure in a play that is not, in theory, supposed to center about him. Shylock's scenes are gripping and fascinating, and many critics believe the play deflates every time he makes an exit.

2.   *In the end, how comic is* THE MERCHANT OF VENICE? *Does the final act succeed in restoring comedy to the play?*

The Merchant of Venice contains all of the elements required of a Shakespearean comedy, but is often so overshadowed by the character of Shylock and his quest for a pound of flesh that it is hard not to find in the play a generous share of the tragic as well. Lovers pine and are reunited, a foolish servant makes endless series of puns, and genteel women masquerade as men—all of which are defining marks of Shakespearean comedy. In sharp contrast to these elements, however, Shakespeare also presents Shylock, a degraded old man who has lost his daughter and is consumed with a bloody greed. The light language of the play's comedic moments disappears for whole scenes at a time, and Antonio's fate is more suspenseful than funny. The final act redeems the play's claims to be a comedy, piling on the necessary humor and serendipity, but the rest of the play is overcast by the fact that Antonio may soon pay Bassanio's debt with his life.

3.   *Discuss the relationship between Jessica and Shylock. Are we meant to sympathize with the moneylender's daughter? Does Shakespeare seem ambivalent in his portrayal of Jessica?*

In looking at the relationship between Jessica and Shylock, we are again forced to walk a fine line between sympathizing with and despising Shylock. For all intents and purposes, the play should label Shylock's mistreatment by his own daughter as richly deserved. After all, he is spiteful, petty, and mean, and in his more cartoonish or evil moments, it is hard to imagine why Jessica should stay. At other times, however, Jessica's escape seems like another cruel circumstance inflicted on Shylock, and her behavior offstage borders on heartless. Shylock is never more sympathetic than when he bemoans the fact that Jessica has taken a ring given to him in his bachelor days by his wife and has traded it for a monkey, the most banal of objects. Nor is Jessica ever able to produce satisfactory evidence that life in her father's house is miserable. Her seeming indifference to Antonio's fate—she and Lorenzo are more interested in the price of bacon—makes us wonder whether Jessica is actually more selfish and self-absorbed than the father she condemns. While Shylock is no saint, his resolve to collect his debt only seems to strengthen beyond reason after he discovers that Jessica has fled.

How to Write Literary Analysis

The Literary Essay: A Step-by-Step Guide

When you read for pleasure, your only goal is enjoyment. You might find yourself reading to get caught up in an exciting story, to learn about an interesting time or place, or just to pass time. Maybe you're looking for inspiration, guidance, or a reflection of your own life. There are as many different, valid ways of reading a book as there are books in the world.

When you read a work of literature in an English class, however, you're being asked to read in a special way: you're being asked to perform *literary analysis*. To analyze something means to break it down into smaller parts and then examine how those parts work, both individually and together. Literary analysis involves examining all the parts of a novel, play, short story, or poem—elements such as character, setting, tone, and imagery—and thinking about how the author uses those elements to create certain effects.

A literary essay isn't a book review: you're not being asked whether or not you liked a book or whether you'd recommend it to another reader. A literary essay also isn't like the kind of book report you wrote when you were younger, where your teacher wanted you to summarize the book's action. A high school- or college-level literary essay asks, "How does this piece of literature actually work?" "How does it do what it does?" and, "Why might the author have made the choices he or she did?"

The Seven Steps

No one is born knowing how to analyze literature; it's a skill you learn and a process you can master. As you gain more practice with this kind of thinking and writing, you'll be able to craft a method that works best for you. But until then, here are seven basic steps to writing a well-constructed literary essay:

1. *Ask questions*
2. *Collect evidence*
3. *Construct a thesis*

4. Develop and organize arguments
5. Write the introduction
6. Write the body paragraphs
7. Write the conclusion

1. ASK QUESTIONS

When you're assigned a literary essay in class, your teacher will often provide you with a list of writing prompts. Lucky you! Now all you have to do is choose one. Do yourself a favor and pick a topic that interests you. You'll have a much better (not to mention easier) time if you start off with something you enjoy thinking about. If you are asked to come up with a topic by yourself, though, you might start to feel a little panicked. Maybe you have too many ideas—or none at all. Don't worry. Take a deep breath and start by asking yourself these questions:

- **What struck you?** Did a particular image, line, or scene linger in your mind for a long time? If it fascinated you, chances are you can draw on it to write a fascinating essay.

- **What confused you?** Maybe you were surprised to see a character act in a certain way, or maybe you didn't understand why the book ended the way it did. Confusing moments in a work of literature are like a loose thread in a sweater: if you pull on it, you can unravel the entire thing. Ask yourself why the author chose to write about that character or scene the way he or she did and you might tap into some important insights about the work as a whole.

- **Did you notice any patterns?** Is there a phrase that the main character uses constantly or an image that repeats throughout the book? If you can figure out how that pattern weaves through the work and what the significance of that pattern is, you've almost got your entire essay mapped out.

- **Did you notice any contradictions or ironies?** Great works of literature are complex; great literary essays recognize and explain those complexities. Maybe the title (*Happy Days*) totally disagrees with the book's subject matter (hungry orphans dying in the woods). Maybe the main character acts one way around his family and a completely different way around his friends and associates. If you can find a way to explain a work's contradictory elements, you've got the seeds of a great essay.

At this point, you don't need to know exactly what you're going to say about your topic; you just need a place to begin your exploration. You can help direct your reading and brainstorming by formulating your topic as a *question,* which you'll then try to answer in your essay. The best questions invite critical debates and discussions, not just a rehashing of the summary. Remember, you're looking for something you can *prove or argue* based on evidence you find in the text. Finally, remember to keep the scope of your question in mind: is this a topic you can adequately address within the word or page limit you've been given? Conversely, is this a topic big enough to fill the required length?

GOOD QUESTIONS

> *"Are Romeo and Juliet's parents responsible for the deaths of their children?"*
> *"Why do pigs keep showing up in* LORD OF THE FLIES*?"*
> *"Are Dr. Frankenstein and his monster alike? How?"*

BAD QUESTIONS

> *"What happens to Scout in* TO KILL A MOCKINGBIRD*?"*
> *"What do the other characters in* JULIUS CAESAR *think about Caesar?"*
> *"How does Hester Prynne in* THE SCARLET LETTER *remind me of my sister?"*

---

2. COLLECT EVIDENCE

Once you know what question you want to answer, it's time to scour the book for things that will help you answer the question. Don't worry if you don't know what you want to say yet—right now you're just collecting ideas and material and letting it all percolate. Keep track of passages, symbols, images, or scenes that deal with your topic. Eventually, you'll start making connections between these examples and your thesis will emerge.

Here's a brief summary of the various parts that compose each and every work of literature. These are the elements that you will analyze in your essay, and which you will offer as evidence to support your arguments. For more on the parts of literary works, see the Glossary of Literary Terms at the end of this section.

LITERARY ANALYSIS

ELEMENTS OF STORY   These are the *what*s of the work—what happens, where it happens, and to whom it happens.

- **Plot:** All of the events and actions of the work.
- **Character:** The people who act and are acted upon in a literary work. The main character of a work is known as the *protagonist.*
- **Conflict:** The central tension in the work. In most cases, the protagonist wants something, while opposing forces (antagonists) hinder the protagonist's progress.
- **Setting:** When and where the work takes place. Elements of setting include location, time period, time of day, weather, social atmosphere, and economic conditions.
- **Narrator:** The person telling the story. The narrator may straightforwardly report what happens, convey the subjective opinions and perceptions of one or more characters, or provide commentary and opinion in his or her own voice.
- **Themes:** The main idea or message of the work—usually an abstract idea about people, society, or life in general. A work may have many themes, which may be in tension with one another.

ELEMENTS OF STYLE   These are the *how*s—how the characters speak, how the story is constructed, and how language is used throughout the work.

- **Structure and organization:** How the parts of the work are assembled. Some novels are narrated in a linear, chronological fashion, while others skip around in time. Some plays follow a traditional three- or five-act structure, while others are a series of loosely connected scenes. Some authors deliberately leave gaps in their works, leaving readers to puzzle out the missing information. A work's structure and organization can tell you a lot about the kind of message it wants to convey.
- **Point of view:** The perspective from which a story is told. In *first-person point of view,* the narrator involves him or herself in the story. ("I went to the store"; "We watched in horror as the bird slammed into the window.") A first-person narrator is usually the protagonist of the work, but not always. In *third-person point of view,* the narrator does not participate

in the story. A third-person narrator may closely follow a specific character, recounting that individual character's thoughts or experiences, or it may be what we call an *omniscient* narrator. Omniscient narrators see and know all: they can witness any event in any time or place and are privy to the inner thoughts and feelings of all characters. Remember that the narrator and the author are not the same thing!

- **Diction:** Word choice. Whether a character uses dry, clinical language or flowery prose with lots of exclamation points can tell you a lot about his or her attitude and personality.

- **Syntax:** Word order and sentence construction. Syntax is a crucial part of establishing an author's narrative voice. Ernest Hemingway, for example, is known for writing in very short, straightforward sentences, while James Joyce characteristically wrote in long, incredibly complicated lines.

- **Tone:** The mood or feeling of the text. Diction and syntax often contribute to the tone of a work. A novel written in short, clipped sentences that use small, simple words might feel brusque, cold, or matter-of-fact.

- **Imagery:** Language that appeals to the senses, representing things that can be seen, smelled, heard, tasted, or touched.

- **Figurative language:** Language that is not meant to be interpreted literally. The most common types of figurative language are *metaphors* and *similes,* which compare two unlike things in order to suggest a similarity between them— for example, "All the world's a stage," or "The moon is like a ball of green cheese." (Metaphors say one thing *is* another thing; similes claim that one thing is *like* another thing.)

---

3. CONSTRUCT A THESIS

When you've examined all the evidence you've collected and know how you want to answer the question, it's time to write your thesis statement. A *thesis* is a claim about a work of literature that needs to be supported by evidence and arguments. The thesis statement is the heart of the literary essay, and the bulk of your paper will be spent trying to prove this claim. A good thesis will be:

- **Arguable.** "*The Great Gatsby* describes New York society in the 1920s" isn't a thesis—it's a fact.

- **Provable through textual evidence**. "*Hamlet* is a confusing but ultimately very well-written play" is a weak thesis because it offers the writer's personal opinion about the book. Yes, it's arguable, but it's not a claim that can be proved or supported with examples taken from the play itself.

- **Surprising**. "Both George and Lenny change a great deal in *Of Mice and Men*" is a weak thesis because it's obvious. A really strong thesis will argue for a reading of the text that is not immediately apparent.

- **Specific.** "Dr. Frankenstein's monster tells us a lot about the human condition" is *almost* a really great thesis statement, but it's still too vague. What does the writer mean by "a lot"? *How* does the monster tell us so much about the human condition?

GOOD THESIS STATEMENTS

Question: In *Romeo and Juliet*, which is more powerful in shaping the lovers' story: fate or foolishness?

Thesis: "Though Shakespeare defines Romeo and Juliet as 'star-crossed lovers' and images of stars and planets appear throughout the play, a closer examination of that celestial imagery reveals that the stars are merely witnesses to the characters' foolish activities and not the causes themselves."

Question: How does the bell jar function as a symbol in Sylvia Plath's *The Bell Jar*?

Thesis: "A bell jar is a bell-shaped glass that has three basic uses: to hold a specimen for observation, to contain gases, and to maintain a vacuum. The bell jar appears in each of these capacities in *The Bell Jar,* Plath's semi-autobiographical novel, and each appearance marks a different stage in Esther's mental breakdown."

Question: Would Piggy in *The Lord of the Flies* make a good island leader if he were given the chance?

Thesis: "Though the intelligent, rational, and innovative Piggy has the mental characteristics of a good leader, he ultimately lacks the social skills necessary to be an effective one. Golding emphasizes this point by giving Piggy a foil in the charismatic Jack, whose magnetic personality allows him to capture and wield power effectively, if not always wisely."

4. Develop and Organize Arguments

The reasons and examples that support your thesis will form the middle paragraphs of your essay. Since you can't really write your thesis statement until you know how you'll structure your argument, you'll probably end up working on steps 3 and 4 at the same time.

There's no single method of argumentation that will work in every context. One essay prompt might ask you to compare and contrast two characters, while another asks you to trace an image through a given work of literature. These questions require different kinds of answers and therefore different kinds of arguments. Below, we'll discuss three common kinds of essay prompts and some strategies for constructing a solid, well-argued case.

Types of Literary Essays

- **Compare and contrast**

  Compare and contrast the characters of Huck and Jim in The Adventures of Huckleberry Finn.

  Chances are you've written this kind of essay before. In an academic literary context, you'll organize your arguments the same way you would in any other class. You can either go *subject by subject* or *point by point*. In the former, you'll discuss one character first and then the second. In the latter, you'll choose several traits (attitude toward life, social status, images and metaphors associated with the character) and devote a paragraph to each. You may want to use a mix of these two approaches—for example, you may want to spend a paragraph apiece broadly sketching Huck's and Jim's personalities before transitioning into a paragraph or two that describes a few key points of comparison. This can be a highly effective strategy if you want to make a counterintuitive argument—that, despite seeming to be totally different, the two objects being compared are actually similar in a very important way (or vice versa). Remember that your essay should reveal something fresh or unexpected about the text, so think beyond the obvious parallels and differences.

- **Trace**

  Choose an image—for example, birds, knives, or eyes—and trace that image throughout Macbeth.

  Sounds pretty easy, right? All you need to do is read the play, underline every appearance of a knife in *Macbeth,* and then list them in your essay in the order they appear, right? Well, not exactly. Your teacher doesn't want a simple catalog of examples. He or she wants to see you make *connections* between those examples—that's the difference between summarizing and analyzing. In the *Macbeth* example above, think about the different contexts in which knives appear in the play and to what effect. In *Macbeth,* there are real knives and imagined knives; knives that kill and knives that simply threaten. Categorize and classify your examples to give them some order. Finally, always keep the overall effect in mind. After you choose and analyze your examples, you should come to some greater understanding about the work, as well as your chosen image, symbol, or phrase's role in developing the major themes and stylistic strategies of that work.

- **Debate**

  Is the society depicted in 1984 good for its citizens?

  In this kind of essay, you're being asked to debate a moral, ethical, or aesthetic issue regarding the work. You might be asked to judge a character or group of characters (*Is Caesar responsible for his own demise?*) or the work itself (*Is* JANE EYRE *a feminist novel?*). For this kind of essay, there are two important points to keep in mind. First, don't simply base your arguments on your personal feelings and reactions. Every literary essay expects you to read and analyze the work, so search for evidence in the text. What do characters in *1984* have to say about the government of Oceania? What images does Orwell use that might give you a hint about his attitude toward the government? As in any debate, you also need to make sure that you define all the necessary terms before you begin to argue your case. What does it mean to be a "good" society? What makes a novel "feminist"? You should define your terms right up front, in the first paragraph after your introduction.

  Second, remember that strong literary essays make contrary and surprising arguments. Try to think outside the box. In the *1984* example above, it seems like the obvious answer would be no, the totalitarian society depicted in Orwell's novel is *not* good for its citizens. But can you think of any arguments for the opposite side? Even if your final assertion is that the novel depicts a cruel, repressive, and therefore harmful society, acknowledging and responding to the counterargument will strengthen your overall case.

5. WRITE THE INTRODUCTION

Your introduction sets up the entire essay. It's where you present your topic and articulate the particular issues and questions you'll be addressing. It's also where you, as the writer, introduce yourself to your readers. A persuasive literary essay immediately establishes its writer as a knowledgeable, authoritative figure.

An introduction can vary in length depending on the overall length of the essay, but in a traditional five-paragraph essay it should be no longer than one paragraph. However long it is, your introduction needs to:

- **Provide any necessary context.** Your introduction should situate the reader and let him or her know what to expect. What book are you discussing? Which characters? What topic will you be addressing?

- **Answer the "So what?" question.** Why is this topic important, and why is your particular position on the topic noteworthy? Ideally, your introduction should pique the reader's interest by suggesting how your argument is surprising or otherwise counterintuitive. Literary essays make unexpected connections and reveal less-than-obvious truths.

- **Present your thesis.** This usually happens at or very near the end of your introduction.

- **Indicate the shape of the essay to come.** Your reader should finish reading your introduction with a good sense of the scope of your essay as well as the path you'll take toward proving your thesis. You don't need to spell out every step, but you do need to suggest the organizational pattern you'll be using.

Your introduction should not:

- **Be vague.** Beware of the two killer words in literary analysis: *interesting* and *important*. Of course the work, question, or example is interesting and important—that's why you're writing about it!

- **Open with any grandiose assertions.** Many student readers think that beginning their essays with a flamboyant statement such as, "Since the dawn of time, writers have been fascinated with the topic of free will," makes them sound important and commanding. You know what? It actually sounds pretty amateurish.

- **Wildly praise the work.** Another typical mistake student writers make is extolling the work or author. Your teacher doesn't need to be told that "Shakespeare is perhaps the greatest writer in the English language." You can mention a work's reputation in passing—by referring to *The Adventures of Huckleberry Finn* as "Mark Twain's enduring classic," for example—but don't make a point of bringing it up unless that reputation is key to your argument.

- **Go off-topic.** Keep your introduction streamlined and to the point. Don't feel the need to throw in all kinds of bells and whistles in order to impress your reader—just get to the point as quickly as you can, without skimping on any of the required steps.

6. WRITE THE BODY PARAGRAPHS

Once you've written your introduction, you'll take the arguments you developed in step 4 and turn them into your body paragraphs. The organization of this middle section of your essay will largely be determined by the argumentative strategy you use, but no matter how you arrange your thoughts, your body paragraphs need to do the following:

- **Begin with a strong topic sentence.** Topic sentences are like signs on a highway: they tell the reader where they are and where they're going. A good topic sentence not only alerts readers to what issue will be discussed in the following paragraph but also gives them a sense of what argument will be made *about* that issue. "Rumor and gossip play an important role in *The Crucible*" isn't a strong topic sentence because it doesn't tell us very much. "The community's constant gossiping creates an environment that allows false accusations to flourish" is a much stronger topic sentence— it not only tells us *what* the paragraph will discuss (gossip) but *how* the paragraph will discuss the topic (by showing how gossip creates a set of conditions that leads to the play's climactic action).

- **Fully and completely develop a single thought.** Don't skip around in your paragraph or try to stuff in too much material. Body paragraphs are like bricks: each individual

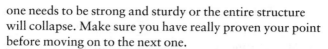

one needs to be strong and sturdy or the entire structure will collapse. Make sure you have really proven your point before moving on to the next one.

- **Use transitions effectively.** Good literary essay writers know that each paragraph must be clearly and strongly linked to the material around it. Think of each paragraph as a response to the one that precedes it. Use transition words and phrases such as *however, similarly, on the contrary, therefore,* and *furthermore* to indicate what kind of response you're making.

---

7. WRITE THE CONCLUSION

Just as you used the introduction to ground your readers in the topic before providing your thesis, you'll use the conclusion to quickly summarize the specifics learned thus far and then hint at the broader implications of your topic. A good conclusion will:

- **Do more than simply restate the thesis.** If your thesis argued that *The Catcher in the Rye* can be read as a Christian allegory, don't simply end your essay by saying, "And that is why *The Catcher in the Rye* can be read as a Christian allegory." If you've constructed your arguments well, this kind of statement will just be redundant.

- **Synthesize the arguments, not summarize them.** Similarly, don't repeat the details of your body paragraphs in your conclusion. The reader has already read your essay, and chances are it's not so long that they've forgotten all your points by now.

- **Revisit the "So what?" question.** In your introduction, you made a case for why your topic and position are important. You should close your essay with the same sort of gesture. What do your readers know now that they didn't know before? How will that knowledge help them better appreciate or understand the work overall?

- **Move from the specific to the general.** Your essay has most likely treated a very specific element of the work—a single character, a small set of images, or a particular passage. In your conclusion, try to show how this narrow discussion has wider implications for the work overall. If your essay on *To Kill a Mockingbird* focused on the character of Boo Radley, for example, you might want to include a bit in your conclusion about how he fits into the novel's larger message about childhood, innocence, or family life.

- **Stay relevant.** Your conclusion should suggest new directions of thought, but it shouldn't be treated as an opportunity to pad your essay with all the extra, interesting ideas you came up with during your brainstorming sessions but couldn't fit into the essay proper. Don't attempt to stuff in unrelated queries or too many abstract thoughts.

- **Avoid making overblown closing statements.** A conclusion should open up your highly specific, focused discussion, but it should do so without drawing a sweeping lesson about life or human nature. Making such observations may be part of the point of reading, but it's almost always a mistake in essays, where these observations tend to sound overly dramatic or simply silly.

A+ Essay Checklist

Congratulations! If you've followed all the steps we've outlined above, you should have a solid literary essay to show for all your efforts. What if you've got your sights set on an A+? To write the kind of superlative essay that will be rewarded with a perfect grade, keep the following rubric in mind. These are the qualities that teachers expect to see in a truly A+ essay. How does yours stack up?

- ✓ Demonstrates a thorough understanding of the book
- ✓ Presents an original, compelling argument
- ✓ Thoughtfully analyzes the text's formal elements
- ✓ Uses appropriate and insightful examples
- ✓ Structures ideas in a logical and progressive order
- ✓ Demonstrates a mastery of sentence construction, transitions, grammar, spelling, and word choice

Suggested Essay Topics

1. *Discuss the relationship between Antonio and Bassanio. What does their friendship reveal about their characters?*

2. *Examine Shylock's rhetoric. Pay special attention to the quality of his language—his use of metaphor and repetition, for instance. How do his speeches reflect his character as a whole?*

3. *Compare and contrast Venice and Belmont. What is the significance of these distinct settings in the play?*

4. *Analyze the way that time passes in* THE MERCHANT OF VENICE, *paying special attention to conflicts between time in Venice and Belmont. Are there any inconsistencies, and if so, how does the play handle them?*

5. *To what extent is Shylock defined by his Jewishness? To what extent is he defined by his profession?*

6. *Discuss Portia's character. How does she compare to the men around her? Is Bassanio a worthy husband for her?*

A+ STUDENT ESSAY

Examine the courtroom scene in *The Merchant of Venice*.
How does it illuminate the play's major themes?

Shakespeare's courtroom scene dramatizes a conflict between justice and mercy—the competing claims of an angry Shylock and a desperate Bassanio. This argument mirrors several smaller disputes and personal crises throughout *The Merchant of Venice*. Shakespeare's characters must frequently weigh their sense of grievance against their sense of generosity. By placing the conflict at the center of his play, Shakespeare suggests that the pains of sacrifice are inescapable. It is human to resent, and it is human to forgive.

The courtroom scene enacts a crisis all humans must someday face: whether to pardon an enemy or insist on revenge. Portia speaks on behalf of mercy, arguing that we must always forgive one another because we are constantly hoping for our own share of forgiveness from an all-knowing God. Likewise, the Duke demonstrates the virtues of mercy when he ignores the letter of the law and waves away his right to take Shylock's life. On the other hand, Shylock represents the all-too-human desire for justice. He has evidence of Antonio's oath and simply wants to carry out the terms of the agreement. Portia frightens him when she begins to argue in Shylock's own terms. Invoking the supremacy of justice, she says he may have a pound of flesh but not a drop of blood, with the threatened penalty of death if he does not follow her terms exactly. Mercy and justice—forgiveness and vengeance—spar relentlessly in this climactic scene.

Shakespeare has laid the thematic groundwork for his climax by repeatedly noting the virtues of a merciful way of life. Antonio takes on heroic stature when he forgives Bassanio's countless debts and encourages him to find love. Portia tempers Nerissa's severity when she says we must be merciful unto others as well as unto ourselves. Portia forgives Bassanio for leaving Belmont on the night of their engagement, putting aside her own wishes and encouraging him to help his friend. Jessica and Lorenzo repeatedly note the necessity of good humor; it is in the nature of lovers to stray and to make false promises, so we must try to laugh and see what is best in one another. Each of these characters acts as an occasional spokesperson for the mild-mannered, magnanimous approach to life.

On the other hand, several of Shakespeare's characters crave justice in moments of weakness. Despite his constant sacrifices, Antonio becomes irritating when he seems to brood on his sense of perpetual martyrdom, and Gratiano urges him to abandon his silent grievances and enjoy his life. Long before the courtroom scene, Shylock embodies the human desire for revenge, asking why he should cooperate with Antonio when Antonio has ignored him and called him a cur. The Prince of Arragon seems absurd when he claims Portia on the grounds that he deserves her, and the message in the silver casket rebukes him for thinking that we are ever naturally entitled to happiness. In our discomfort and self-absorption, we make the error of Shakespeare's characters and insist on justice in a patently unjust world.

By pitting mercy against justice in his climactic scene, Shakespeare suggests that everyone struggles with competing urges to complain and forgive. Shylock demands the flesh the law has promised him, and Portia argues that the world is too complex to be governed by rigid laws. Portia, Antonio, and Lorenzo all occasionally look past their own problems and behave generously, whereas other characters cannot overcome a gnawing sense of grievance and injustice. In five tolerant, effortless acts, Shakespeare shows us that we are destined to have these arguments—with others and with ourselves—every day of our lives.

LITERARY ANALYSIS

GLOSSARY OF LITERARY TERMS

ANTAGONIST

The entity that acts to frustrate the goals of the *protagonist*. The antagonist is usually another *character* but may also be a non-human force.

ANTIHERO / ANTIHEROINE

A *protagonist* who is not admirable or who challenges notions of what should be considered admirable.

CHARACTER

A person, animal, or any other thing with a personality that appears in a *narrative*.

CLIMAX

The moment of greatest intensity in a text or the major turning point in the *plot*.

CONFLICT

The central struggle that moves the *plot* forward. The conflict can be the *protagonist*'s struggle against fate, nature, society, or another person.

FIRST-PERSON POINT OF VIEW

A literary style in which the *narrator* tells the story from his or her own *point of view* and refers to himself or herself as "I." The narrator may be an active participant in the story or just an observer.

HERO / HEROINE

The principal *character* in a literary work or *narrative*.

IMAGERY

Language that brings to mind sense-impressions, representing things that can be seen, smelled, heard, tasted, or touched.

MOTIF

A recurring idea, structure, contrast, or device that develops or informs the major *themes* of a work of literature.

NARRATIVE

A story.

NARRATOR

The person (sometimes a *character*) who tells a story; the *voice* assumed by the writer. The narrator and the author of the work of literature are not the same person.

PLOT

The arrangement of the events in a story, including the sequence in which they are told, the relative emphasis they are given, and the causal connections between events.

POINT OF VIEW

The *perspective* that a *narrative* takes toward the events it describes.

PROTAGONIST

The main *character* around whom the story revolves.

SETTING

The location of a *narrative* in time and space. Setting creates mood or atmosphere.

SUBPLOT

A secondary *plot* that is of less importance to the overall story but may serve as a point of contrast or comparison to the main plot.

SYMBOL

An object, *character,* figure, or color that is used to represent an abstract idea or concept. Unlike an *emblem,* a symbol may have different meanings in different contexts.

SYNTAX

The way the words in a piece of writing are put together to form lines, phrases, or clauses; the basic structure of a piece of writing.

THEME

A fundamental and universal idea explored in a literary work.

TONE

The author's attitude toward the subject or *characters* of a story or poem or toward the reader.

VOICE

An author's individual way of using language to reflect his or her own personality and attitudes. An author communicates voice through *tone, diction*, and *syntax*.

A Note on Plagiarism

Plagiarism—presenting someone else's work as your own—rears its ugly head in many forms. Many students know that copying text without citing it is unacceptable. But some don't realize that even if you're not quoting directly, but instead are paraphrasing or summarizing, *it is plagiarism* unless you cite the source.

Here are the most common forms of plagiarism:

- Using an author's phrases, sentences, or paragraphs without citing the source
- Paraphrasing an author's ideas without citing the source
- Passing off another student's work as your own

How do you steer clear of plagiarism? You should *always* acknowledge all words and ideas that aren't your own by using quotation marks around verbatim text or citations like footnotes and endnotes to note another writer's ideas. For more information on how to give credit when credit is due, ask your teacher for guidance or visit www.sparknotes.com.

REVIEW & RESOURCES

QUIZ

1. What reason does Antonio give for being sad in the opening scene of the play?

   A. He stands to lose a fortune in his present business ventures.
   B. He owes a fantastic sum of money to Shylock.
   C. He gives no reason.
   D. The woman he loves does not return his feelings.

2. From what character flaw does Bassanio believe Gratiano suffers?

   A. Mean-spiritedness
   B. A lack of depth
   C. Stinginess
   D. Vanity

3. The caskets that Portia's suitors must pick from are made of what materials?

   A. Gold, silver, lead
   B. Teak, mahogany, pine
   C. Bone, porcelain, clay
   D. Marble, stone, brick

4. Which of the following is not a reason Shylock gives for hating Antonio?

   A. Antonio is in love with Shylock's daughter, Jessica.
   B. Antonio has insulted Shylock in the past.
   C. Antonio lends money without interest, which damages Shylock's business.
   D. Antonio hates Jews.

5. How does Shylock initially describe his demand for a pound of flesh to Bassanio and Antonio?

   A.   As an opportunity for revenge
   B.   As his way of being charitable
   C.   As a harmless prank
   D.   As a way of procuring food

6. Why does the prince of Morocco fear that Portia will dislike him?

   A.   He is a braggart.
   B.   He has a dark complexion.
   C.   He recently proved a coward in battle.
   D.   His clothes are flamboyant.

7. Whom does Bassanio agree to bring with him to Belmont?

   A.   Old Gobbo
   B.   Gratiano
   C.   Antonio
   D.   Jessica

8. What act does Jessica believe will solve the misery of life with Shylock?

   A.   Becoming a more devout Jew
   B.   Ensuring that Shylock loses his bond to Antonio
   C.   Locking herself in her room
   D.   Marrying Lorenzo

9. According to Lorenzo's plan, how will Jessica escape from her father's house?

   A.   She will disguise herself as Lorenzo's torchbearer and slip out undetected.
   B.   She will leave during the night, while Shylock is asleep.
   C.   She will take her father to a large public auction and get lost in the crowd.
   D.   She will fake her own death.

10. How does Shylock react to losing Launcelot as a servant?

    A.   He weeps in private

    B.   He tells Launcelot that Bassanio will be a harder master

    C.   He beats Launcelot with a stick

    D.   He refuses to pay Launcelot the wages he owes him

11. How does Portia react to the prince of Morocco's failure as a suitor?

    A.   She prays that no one with such dark skin ever wins her hand.

    B.   She is relieved because the quick-tempered prince would not have made a stable husband.

    C.   She is sad to lose such a wealthy suitor.

    D.   She laughs at his foolishness and sends him away.

12. Who loses the opportunity to marry Portia by choosing the silver casket?

    A.   The Jew of Malta

    B.   The prince of Arragon

    C.   The duke of Earl

    D.   The viscount of Normandy

13. According to Tubal's report, for what did Jessica trade Shylock's most precious ring?

    A.   A gondola

    B.   A horse for Bassanio

    C.   A christening gown for her first child

    D.   A monkey

14. What course of action does Portia suggest when she learns that Shylock wishes to collect his pound of flesh?

    A.   That Bassanio and his men disguise themselves and usher Antonio a safe distance away from Venice

    B.   That the matter be dealt with in a court of law

    C.   That Jessica plead with her father for mercy

    D.   That the bond be paid many times over

REVIEW & RESOURCES

15. Where does Portia instruct her servant Balthasar to hurry?

   A. To an apothecary
   B. To Padua to visit Doctor Bellario
   C. To Morocco
   D. To Shylock's house

16. What complaint does Launcelot make regarding the conversion of the Jews?

   A. He says there would be no one left to loan money.
   B. He says the garment industry would suffer.
   C. He says that the price of bacon would soar.
   D. He says the Catholic Church would be unable to handle so many conversions.

17. In court, how does Antonio react to Shylock's insistence on collecting his pound of flesh?

   A. He weeps openly.
   B. He vows that he will meet Shylock's hatred with patience.
   C. He curses Shylock's vengefulness.
   D. He makes an impassioned plea to the court to intervene on his behalf.

18. Who enters the court disguised as a young doctor of Law named Balthasar?

   A. Portia
   B. Nerissa
   C. Jessica
   D. Lorenzo

19. What loophole in Shylock's bond allows Portia to stop him from taking a pound of Antonio's flesh?

   A. Jewish law prohibits Shylock from practicing his trade on the Sabbath.
   B. Shylock is entitled only to flesh, but not blood.
   C. Shylock forgot to sign the bond.
   D. There is no hard evidence that Antonio's ships have sunk, and that he cannot pay the bond.

20. How is Shylock punished for seeking to take Antonio's life?

   A.   He is banished.
   B.   He is ordered to surrender all his property to the Church of Rome.
   C.   He must convert to Christianity and will his possessions to Jessica and Lorenzo upon his death.
   D.   He must work as Antonio's servant for the remainder of his life.

21. What words does Shylock utter after accepting the court's sentence?

   A.   A pox upon Venice
   B.   These are most unlawful laws
   C.   Forgive me my sins
   D.   I am not well

22. What does Bassanio offer the young law clerk who saves Antonio?

   A.   His gloves
   B.   His wife
   C.   The ring that Portia gave him
   D.   The three thousand ducats originally due to Shylock

23. What does Lorenzo order when he learns that Portia is on her way to Belmont?

   A.   A banquet to welcome the lady of the house
   B.   Music
   C.   A ring to match the one she once gave to Bassanio
   D.   Flowers

24. What does Portia vow to do when she learns that Bassanio no longer has the ring she gave him?

   A.   Never again speak to her husband
   B.   Deny her husband children
   C.   Leave her husband
   D.   Make her husband a cuckold

25. What news does Antonio receive at the play's end?

   A. Shylock has killed himself.
   B. Some of the ships he supposed were lost have arrived in port.
   C. The duke of Venice has changed his mind and finds Antonio guilty of forfeiture of Shylock's bond.
   D. His long lost brother has been found.

Suggestions for Further Reading

AUDEN, W. H. "Brothers & Others." In *The Dyer's Hand and Other Essays*, 218–237. New York: Random House, 1962.

GROSS, JOHN. *Shylock: A Legend and Its Legacy.* New York: Simon and Schuster, 1992.

HOLMER, JOAN OZARK. THE MERCHANT OF VENICE: *Choice, Hazard, and Consequence.* Basingstoke, Hampshire: Macmillan, 1995.

KAPLAN, M. LINDSAY. THE MERCHANT OF VENICE: *Texts and Contexts.* New York: Bedford/St. Martin's, 2002.

MAHON, JOHN W. and ELLEN MACLEOD MAHON. THE MERCHANT OF VENICE: *New Critical Essays.* London: Routledge, 2002.

SHAPIRO, JAMES S. *Shakespeare and the Jews.* New York: Columbia University Press, 1996.

SPENCER, CHRISTOPHER. *The Genesis of Shakespeare's* MERCHANT OF VENICE. Lewiston, New York: E. Mellen Press, 1988.

SMITH, EMMA. *The Cambridge Introduction to Shakespeare.* Cambridge: Cambridge University Press, 2007.